DEVIL'S ADVOCATES

T0373118

DEVIL'S ADVOCATES is a series of books devoted to exploring the classics of horror cinema. Contributors to the series come from the fields of teaching, academia, journalism and fiction, but all have one thing in common: a passion for the horror film and a desire to share it with the widest possible audience.

'The admirable Devil's Advocates series is not only essential – and fun – reading for the serious horror fan but should be set texts on any genre course.'
Dr Ian Hunter, Reader in Film Studies, De Montfort University, Leicester

'Auteur Publishing's new Devil's Advocates critiques on individual titles... offer bracingly fresh perspectives from passionate writers. The series will perfectly complement the BFI archive volumes.' **Christopher Fowler, *Independent on Sunday***

'Devil's Advocates has proven itself more than capable of producing impassioned, intelligent analyses of genre cinema... quickly becoming the go-to guys for intelligent, easily digestible film criticism.' *Horror Talk.com*

'Auteur Publishing continue the good work of giving serious critical attention to significant horror films.' ***Black Static***

 DevilsAdvocatesbooks

 DevilsAdBooks

DEVIL'S ADVOCATES

THE WICKER MAN

STEVE A. WIGGINS

ACKNOWLEDGMENTS

My thanks go out to John Atkinson of Auteur/LUP for believing in this project from the beginning and for sage advice along the path. The anonymous reviewers helped to improve the book in many ways. Thanks to Kelly Murphy at Central Michigan University, Tanya Krzywinska of Falmouth University, Marion Gibson of Exeter University, and Diane Rodgers of Sheffield Hallam University for supplying me with materials to which I would not otherwise have had access. My thanks to Brandon Grafius for pointing Devil's Advocates out to me in the first place and to Doug Cowan for showing how it's done. Kay and Kietra, as always, stood behind my strange obsession while I wrote. My profound thanks to you all.

First published in 2023 by
Auteur, an imprint of
Liverpool University Press,
4 Cambridge Street,
Liverpool
L69 7ZU

Series design: Nikki Hamlett at Cassels Design
Set by Cassels Design, Luton UK
Printed and bound by CPI Group (UK) Ltd, Croydon CR0 4YY

British Library Cataloguing-in-Publication Data
A catalogue record for this book is available from the British Library

ISBN hardback: 978-1-83764-466-7
ISBN paperback: 978-1-83764-388-2
eISBN: 978-1-83764-492-6

CONTENTS

FIGURES

INTRODUCTION

Sergeant Howie is losing his temper. Not only are the citizens of Summerisle obviously lying to him about the missing Rowan Morrison, but they're openly celebrating pagan rituals in the twentieth century. He doesn't trust them. They don't share his worldview. Since his arrival on this isolated Scottish island he's witnessed rowdiness in the tavern, couples making love in full view outdoors, schoolchildren being taught "immoral" lessons, and young ladies dancing naked around a fire. Now Lord Summerisle, the local authority, is treating this as if it's all completely normal. What of Christianity? Summerisle explains how his grandfather purchased the island and reinstated the old religion. His son continued the legacy. Howie, exasperated, declares, "He brought you up to be a pagan!" The note of accusation in his voice is clear.

Calmly, with just a hint of menace, Lord Summerisle almost smiles as he turns toward the camera and replies, "A heathen, conceivably, but not, I hope, an unenlightened one."

The first interview between Sgt. Howie and Lord Summerisle demonstrates the clash of religious worlds around the holiday of May Day presented in *The Wicker Man* (Robin Hardy, 1973). Seasoned viewers know that Howie has been set up and that he'll be reduced to sitting in a small chair at the local library to research this unfamiliar holiday on the day of his death. Even repeat viewers may not, however, realize they're seeing a textbook example of holiday horror.

If you're reading this book you have probably already had your appointment with *The Wicker Man*. You know that it was directed by Robin Hardy and written by Anthony Shaffer. You know that it stars Edward Woodward as Sergeant Neil Howie of the West Highland Constabulary and Christopher Lee as Lord Summerisle. You know that Willow MacGregor (Britt Ekland) has a memorable nude dancing scene and that the overall movie is intelligent, low-budget, and quirky. You also know that Howie has been lured as a May Day sacrifice to restore the failed crops of Summerisle. You know he's burnt alive in the eponymous wicker man. You probably also know that the theatrical version is missing about fourteen minutes of the director's cut and that three different versions are in circulation. So why, then, knowing all this, should you read this book?

Building on what you already know, I hope to enhance your appreciation of *The Wicker Man* by setting it in the sub-genre of holiday horror. The film has been analyzed as folk horror, indeed as one of the "unholy trinity" of that sub-genre (Scovell, 2017: 11–15). Yes, folk horror will also be part of the discussion—most films admit to being of more than one sub-genre—but the main angle of approach will be holiday horror. I hope to demonstrate how *The Wicker Man* became a cult classic, even with its famous distribution problems, by effectively utilizing holiday horror as a vehicle. This sheds light on how a film that almost vanished in obscurity has come to be called "the *Citizen Kane* of horror films" (Bartholomew, 1977: 5) and hailed as a classic of British filmmaking. It does this by tapping into religion openly, splaying out the fear religion engenders for all to see. There's little supernatural about *The Wicker Man*. It could really happen if people took their religion completely literally (although some of the continuity problems will be discussed below). As the influence of religion continues to grow more aggressive in politics, indeed, it becomes easier to imagine.

The movie as analyzed in this book is the 88-minute original theatrical version. While the 102-minute full version (the director's cut) is now available, the original theatrical version has become a classic in its own right and is widely recognized.[1] Also, the director's cut changes the timing of some of the action. To make sense of a "text" we must all have the same version in front of us. Not only that, but as I have argued elsewhere, longer cuts (and sequels) change the story (Wiggins, 2018). We need to agree on which story we're talking about. There is a case to be made for using the director's cut since it has further explanation and background, but those familiar with this longer version can still make sense of the original theatrical release, the focus of this book. The version that most first-time viewers see, and which draws them into fandom, is the theatrical release. It is our "text" here.

I will make use of interviews in documentaries and compilations to get to some of the facts or traditions behind this complex film. The story begins with a novel—*Ritual*, by David Pinner—which has subsequently become a collector's item. A novelization was also written after the movie was released. There are complexities at every level. For this film those complexities began with a red-letter day.

TIMING

This book isn't the first to study *The Wicker Man*.[2] Others have probed the genre, cinematography, and even the famous production and distribution woes of the film. It has been analyzed as subversive horror (Murray and Rolston, 2008) and folk horror (Scovell, 2017; Paciorek et al., 2018), both of which clearly fit the movie. Since this book uses the primary lens of holiday horror, these other interpretative approaches will fall into the background. Many angles are helpful in understanding this complex film. There will be spoilers in this book, so if you haven't yet had your appointment with the wicker man, please make one before reading further.

One curious feature of more than one previous analysis is the claim that the film is set in 1972 (Brown, 2000: xix–xx; Murray and Rolston, 2008: 4). It is worth taking a moment at the start to state that although released in October of 1973, and filmed in late autumn and early winter of 1972, the film is set on May Day of 1973. This is made clear from the moment Sgt. Howie notices that the May Day photo from 1972 is missing in the Green Man.[3] He asks Mr. Lennox (Donald Eccles) about "last year's photo," only to be told there is no copy. If last year's May Queen harvest photo was taken in 1972, then the current setting in which Howie is investigating logically has to be 1973, since it's currently late April. That means that the film was initially presented as contemporary to 1973, the year of its release. Also, the calendar in Scene 92 (in Shaffer's script), where Howie is developing and printing the missing photo, plainly reads May 1973. The date is important in reading the film.

Figure 1. Note the year. © British Lion

Horror films often use the convention of contemporaneity, creating fear that the danger remains out there now. Just a couple examples will suffice. *Children of the Corn* (Fritz Kiersch, 1984), based on a Stephen King short story, sets itself in the "present day." The fear that such rogue children may be lurking in Nebraska accompanies viewers from the theater.[4] A second example is *The Blair Witch Project* (Daniel Myrick and Eduardo Sánchez, 1999). Framed as "found footage," the *cinéma vérité* style suggests that Heather, Michael, and Joshua are missing right now, at the moment you're watching the film. This kind of verisimilitude gives horror a particular relevancy and adds to that lingering worry, did this really happen? Is it happening still? Does such a ritual really exist?

RELATING TO *RITUAL*

The novel *Ritual* was published by David Pinner in 1967. It didn't become a runaway success, but it caught the attention of a group of British filmmakers (Catterall and Wells, 2001: 124–25). Christopher Lee, who hardly requires an introduction, had grown famous as a star in Hammer horror films. Although lucrative, Hammer horror was somewhat formulaic, often reshooting the same monsters that others had brought to the screen, such as Dracula and Frankenstein's creature. According to interviews with those involved in *The Wicker Man*,[5] Lee approached screenwriter Anthony Shaffer about making a more intelligent film with him. Shaffer recollected that he was also asked to keep his friend and business partner Robin Hardy quiet after a heart attack. Shaffer did this by bringing Hardy library books about the occult history of the British Isles (*Wicker Man Enigma*).

Although Pinner's novel was fairly recent at that time, those involved seem quickly to have forgotten it (Bartholomew, 1977: 9). Shaffer had read *Ritual* and it was used as a high-level base story for the film Lee, Shaffer, Hardy, and Peter Snell, the head of British Lion at the time, started discussing.[6]

There are significant differences between the novel and the movie. Location is one: the ritual murders in the book take place in Thorn, Cornwall, not the Hebrides. While Thorn is isolated, it's an easy train ride from London. In fact, the police arrive and save the day just that way. (In a sense. The novel has its own twist ending, quite different from the movie.) The folk horror element of isolation sees Sgt. Howie a long plane ride from the mainland in *The Wicker Man*.

There's a *Lord of the Flies*-type gang of kids involved in the scenario in *Ritual*, and although detective David Hanlin detests paganism, he's not particularly religious himself. Pinner calls him "Puritan" several times, but his inner dialogue belies that designation. Anna Spark, who transforms into Willow in the film, does try to seduce Hanlin. One reason he gives for not falling to temptation is that it's afternoon. He thinks at midnight, perhaps he would sleep with her, a thought which no Puritan would consider. Hanlin survives the story, unlike Howie, and Anna does not, unlike Willow.

The novel's final twist is that Hanlin is schizophrenic and was the murderer of Anna Spark, and perhaps one of the children. Throughout the novel he fears satanic sacrifice and ritual murder are taking place in Thorn. This latter theme will be carried over into *The Wicker Man*, but the concept of sacrifice will be much more plainly in view, as well as intentionally carried out rather than being a delusion. Hanlin isn't lured to Thorn and he isn't killed there.

The perceived threat in the novel is witchcraft, and there's some evidence of the supernatural, if it's not all a delusion of Hanlin's illness. The ending of the novel complicates any interpretation of what is actually afoot in Thorn. There is a festival that upsets the officer, but he's not been set up by the villagers. They really do, it seems, want him to leave.

The Wicker Man is far more focused on the holiday than *Ritual*. The stories are, at least on a high level, similar. Recollections of those involved suggest that Hardy, Lee, Shaffer, and Snell were familiar with *Ritual*. Whether it was the basis for the story or the mere inspiration behind it can't be determined with any precision. Interestingly, however, the holiday being celebrated in *Ritual* is Midsummer, not May Day. To get to the importance of this to the film, we need to consider more precisely what holiday horror is.

HOLIDAY HORROR

It's October. In America, normally respectable homes in quiet neighborhoods are festooned with artificial cobwebs, plastic skeletons, Styrofoam gravestones, and a variety of monsters lurking across the lawn. Among fans of Halloween, it has become a month of watching a horror film each day. Somewhere in those 31 days John Carpenter's *Halloween* (1978) will inevitably show up. American thoughts, it seems, turn to horror around this particular holiday. Although *Halloween* is an iconic example of holiday horror, it's not the earliest such film. Nor is Halloween the only holiday featured in this sub-genre of movies. What exactly is a holiday?

Holidays began differently than vacations. Historically, in British usage "vacation" meant time away from school; leisure travel was called a "holiday." American usage expanded the concept of "vacation" to cover non-work travel or even just days off of work. Holidays, in American parlance, are days everyone in a company gets off work because they're widely recognized "red-letter days." Holiday horror can encompass both usages of the word "holiday," but as it was originally defined the focus rests primarily on special days, often with a religious background.[7] The word derives from the combination of "holy" and "day." The category might include other periods of liminal time—time that falls out of the secular into the numinous when unusual or unexpected things happen.

Holiday horror is a sub-genre of the horror film. Sometimes it's a sub-genre of folk horror, as it is here. Classifying movies into genres is an artificial practice in many ways (Tudor, 1974: 135–45; Decker, 2021). The term "horror movie" was coined in 1931 so that Universal executives could wrap their heads around the unexpected success of Tod Browning's *Dracula* and James Whale's *Frankenstein*, both released that year. There had been earlier forms of horror film, of course (Phillips, 2018; Rhodes, 2018). Soon the concept of the horror movie caught on. Auteurs and production companies specializing in the genre appeared. Alfred Hitchcock produced thrillers and horror that built his reputation. Vincent Price would become a household name because of the genre. In Britain, Hammer Film Productions produced hit after hit, now considered classics in the field. The horror genre flourished (Hutchings, 2021).

Horror suffered from a lowbrow reputation, however. It was routinely overlooked at various cinematic award ceremonies. Film critics tended to dismiss it. Even academics rarely paid it much mind. When a critical mass of hundreds of films worthy of comment was reached, the higher education world could no longer ignore it. By the 1990s respectable academic presses were beginning to publish studies on horror films. By two decades later, it was clear that different sub-genres existed within the overarching genre. These, of course, had to be labeled. Slashers were easy enough to spot, but what of other films, such as *The Innocents* (Jack Clayton, 1961), which was more of a moody, gothic film? Or something like *Rosemary's Baby* (Roman Polanski, 1968), with its heavy theological freight? Clearly, horror comes in different varieties.

The horror genre has been questioned in the case of *The Wicker Man*, although generally it's understood in that category. Genre assignments are somewhat flexible and are often hybrids (Decker, 2021). Drama, thriller, and horror overlap. Each category, however, has different types into which it might be further divided and classified. There are many sub-genres under horror as well, and they help to give an idea of how any particular movie is understood, relative to other films.

Two particular sub-genres fit *The Wicker Man* especially well. One is the now widely recognized sub-genre of folk horror (Scovell, 2017; Paciorek et al., 2018). The second has been only more recently proposed—the sub-genre of holiday horror. As the name implies, holiday horror focuses on holidays that give the movie its theme or energy. While the most obvious of these films are identified by their titles—think *Halloween*, *My Bloody Valentine* (George Mihalka, 1981), or *Black Christmas* (Bob Clark, 1974)—that isn't always the case. Movies that fit the category best are those that find the holiday as the source of the horror, and occasionally, the folk religions that in turn fuel those holidays.

Religion. Embarrassing, isn't it? We live in what is perhaps both the least and the most religious period in history. Organized religion is in decline, and yet evangelical Protestantism controls national politics in countries such as the United States. Academic appointments in religious studies have been in steep decline as well. All of this may seem to make religion an unusual angle from which to approach horror.

Religion itself is not so much in decline as it is in transformation. Surveys indicate that "Nones"—those who declare no religious affiliation—are quickly increasing. This, alongside the fact that "spiritual but not religious" is a common self-identification, corroborates what some evolutionary scientists hypothesize: people evolved to be religious. Turned the other way around, religion has had survival benefits and it remains important to people. Religion has its hooks in us, but we don't like to talk about it. That discomfort pervades *The Wicker Man*. And *The Wicker Man* revolves around the pagan holiday of May Day. This makes it holiday horror. Let's look more closely.

NOTES

1. Even these running times are up for debate, as a glance at Brown (2000), Murray and Rolston (2008), and the back of a DVD case or two demonstrates. Some of this is due to projection rates.

2. The main sources are Brown (2000), Franks et al. (2007), Murray and Rolston (2008), and Scovell (2017). It is treated discretely as well in other cinematic sources listed in the bibliography.

3. "The Final Cut" (see below) begins with an opening card reading "Sunday—The 29th of April 1973."

4. *Children of the Corn* could be profitably compared with *The Wicker Man* as folk horror as well. The novel *Ritual*, as we'll see shortly, has children playing a large role in the horror, even though the ending of the novel subverts all of it.

5. Specifically, *The Wicker Man Enigma* documentary (David Gregory, 2001).

6. Brown (2000). Like much else with the film there's some controversy regarding the reconstruction of events. It is true that references to *Ritual* are few, if not entirely absent, in discussions and interviews with Robin Hardy regarding the origins of the movie.

7. One of the most deliberate attempts to systematize different kinds of horror is Vander Kaay and Fernandez-Vander Kaay (2016).

Chapter 1: Holiday Horror

Willow MacGregor visits Sgt. Howie's room with breakfast. She makes it clear why she'd invited him to her room the previous night, and ascertains that he's a committed virgin until marriage. She affirms he should leave that day. "You wouldn't want to be around here on May Day. Not the way you feel," she warns.

Holiday horror is nothing new. Arguably it could date back earlier than celluloid adaptations of Charles Dickens' *A Christmas Carol* (*Scrooge, or Marley's Ghost* appeared in 1901). Instead of a jolly Father Christmas or Santa Claus, Dickens' holiday features four ghosts and an emotionally isolated old man. In British culture, Christmas has long had pride of place when it comes to scary tales (Johnston, 2015; Rodgers, 2017). There's an important point here: the holiday itself doesn't have to be inherently scary for holiday horror to apply—the movie may cause the holiday to be scary. In America the scary holiday shifted toward Halloween.

Although the sub-genre had several exemplars before *Halloween*, it was John Carpenter's breakout film that brought holiday-themed horror to wide consciousness. There was a notable uptick in holiday horror in the 1980s, most of it focused on Christmas but a fair amount based on Halloween. Carpenter's *Halloween*, apart from featuring the holiday, also represented Laurie Strode (Jamie Lee Curtis) as showing a horror movie—*The Thing from Another World* (Christian Nyby and Howard Hawks, 1951)—to Tommy Doyle (Brian Andrews) on Halloween night.[1] Halloween was suggesting itself as an occasion to watch horror. Many sequels would go on to follow *Halloween*, and a significant reboot, again with Jamie Lee Curtis, appeared in 2007. Christmas still dominates holiday horror, although at this point Halloween is swiftly catching up.

Other holidays are also represented. April Fool's Day, although not a religious holiday, has contributed to the category, as have Thanksgiving and Easter. Thanksgiving and Easter are among the major holidays in the United States, but other festive occasions also appear in holiday horror, including St. Patrick's Day, St. Valentine's Day, and New Year's Day, for example. Holiday horror seems to have found its major audience in the United States—*The Wicker Man* was initially better received across the Atlantic than in its nation of origin.[2] Very occasionally a movie about old, pre-Christian European holidays becomes part of the canon. Think *Midsommar* (Ari Aster, 2019). Think *The Wicker Man*.

The point of all of this is that holiday horror has a critical mass of films to be considered a viable sub-genre. Well over a hundred horror films can be classified in the category. If current trends advance it will only continue to grow.

SUB-GENRES

Horror films that feature holidays are as obvious as the leather mask on your face, but it was only in the 2010s that the phrase "holiday horror" really came into circulation. Having caught the interest of academics by then, horror was correctly understood to be an extremely expansive label. Efforts began to bring sharper focus to the genre. One way to do this is to break horror down into its component parts.

Perhaps the most notable effort in this was undertaken by Chris Vander Kaay and Kathleen Fernandez-Vander Kaay. Their 2016 book, *Horror Films by Subgenre: A Viewer's Guide*, lists 70 sub-genres, many of which overlap. Their scheme isn't comprehensive— as long as movies continue to be made and analyzed there will continue to be new types and new categorizations. For example, folk horror doesn't appear in their list. It's important to remember that while genre is a useful categorizing principle, it's frequently an outside system applied to literature, music, or films, for purposes of directing consumers to the products they like. A horror film may participate in several sub-genres; indeed, disagreements about whether a film classifies as horror or not are common. What distinguishes "horror" from a "thriller"? Some science fiction is also horror-themed—the *Alien* franchise, for example. IMDb lists some horror as "drama" and some as "adventure." When genre becomes some kind of sacred decree, not only does it stifle creativity, it also prevents fresh interpretations of worthy movies.

But back to the Vander Kaays. Holiday horror is present among their impressive categorization scheme. They consider the defining elements as themed murders/kills and "A Bad History with the Day" (99). With these brief criteria alone *The Wicker Man* fits, but I would suggest a further refinement of the sub-genre—the holiday is more than incidental to the horror. A horror film can be set on a holiday and not really draw its fear from that particular day. In *Wicker Man* the horror emphasis of May Day lies in the implication that it is the day on which in the past sacrifices were made. The people of Summerisle know what's required to fix their poor harvest of the prior year. The holiday suggests the horrifying solution. Some holiday horror films could have been set at a different time of year, or not necessarily on a holiday, but if holiday horror's fear energy comes from the day itself—remember, most holiday horror occurs on holidays with religious roots—moving it to a different day changes it into something else. Consider again Pinner's *Ritual*.

The novel sets the climax on Midsummer. Although Midsummer shares elements with May Day, they have different foci. May Day is the beginning of the planting season, after the danger of a killing frost has passed. Midsummer celebrates the long days and abundance of warmth several weeks later, not so much an effort to ensure a bountiful harvest. This is the driving force behind *Midsommar*.[3] In *Ritual* the main concern of Detective Hanlin is rooting out witchcraft; the holiday is secondary. By making the film holiday-focused, a focal point for the horror concentrates on May Day. Of course, it's a folk celebration.

FOLK HORROR

A second sub-genre that describes *The Wicker Man* particularly well is folk horror. Like holiday horror, folk horror has been around for many years but was only recently classified. Part of the reason for this is that enough examples had to appear to make their common elements clear. Like holiday horror, folk horror was really only identified as a sub-genre in the 2010s, although the term had been used much earlier.[4] Its main elements include the power of nature, the threatening nature of rural landscapes, and isolation, frequently in those rural landscapes (Scovell, 2017; Huckvale, 2018). Although set in nature the real threat often comes from what people, or monsters, do in isolated places.

Once enough examples of folk horror appeared, an early triumvirate, or "unholy trinity," of folk horror films was recognized: *Witchfinder General* (Michael Reeves, 1968), *The Blood on Satan's Claw* (Piers Haggard, 1971), and *The Wicker Man*. These movies all date from the same era and they all focus on the "threat" of non-Christian religion in a rural setting. *Witchfinder General* stands out from the other two by being the earliest and by having some kind of historical basis. Matthew Hopkins (Vincent Price), the antagonist of the movie, was an actual historical person who styled himself "witchfinder general" and who was almost singlehandedly responsible for the witch-trial craze in England (Cabell, 2006; Cooper, 2011). *The Wicker Man* also stands out as being contemporary rather than set in centuries past.

Mark Gatiss, in his *A History of Horror* documentary, noted that folk horror was a short-lived phenomenon toward the end of the British dominance of horror.[5] In 2010, when the documentary aired, that may have been the case, depending on how folk horror's defined. The genre appears to have been revived, especially with the work of directors Robert Eggers and Ari Aster, following a few years after Gatiss' comment. Both of Eggers' first two features, *The Witch* (2015) and *The Lighthouse* (2019), fit into the genre. Ari Aster's *Midsommar* certainly does, and perhaps his *Hereditary* (2018) does as well. Fritz Kiersch's *Children of the Corn* and the Pang brothers' *The Messengers* (2007) qualify. Like most genres, the boundaries can be stretched a bit. "Short-lived" seems to have been merely dormant. Since others have treated *Wicker Man* as folk horror (Scovell, 2017), the focus here is on holiday horror.

HOLIDAY HORROR

Genres are constantly evolving (Todorov and Berrong, 1976: 159–60). The Vander Kaays make the point that the contrast of the joy of a holiday with the violence of the bad history lends holiday horror a particular poignancy. Holiday horror isn't the same as simply setting a horror movie or novel on a particular day; the theme of the holiday has to bleed over. The holiday can't be simply incidental, like *Sleepy Hollow* (Tim Burton, 1999) being set on Halloween—the holiday isn't integral to the plot. Contrast that with *Gremlins* (Joe Dante, 1984). Not only is it set at Christmas, but the gruesome death of Kate's father on Christmas Eve means the holiday is already suspect. For holiday horror the holiday has to participate in the horror itself.

Many examples could be used to populate this category, on a wide variety of holidays throughout the year. Consider *My Bloody Valentine*, or *Bloody New Year* (Norman J. Warren, 1987). Fearsome leprechauns attack on St. Patrick's Day, or a murderous person in a bunny costume at Easter. No holiday is safe.

Something more fundamental is at play here. Holidays are generally sacred occasions, no matter how secular their celebration might be. And this doesn't only apply to holidays with Jewish or Christian origins. Ari Aster's *Midsommar*, widely compared to *The Wicker Man*, concentrates on a pre-Christian European holiday that has a deadly history. In *Midsommar* the suicide of the elders is an expected element of the celebration's bad-day history, while the more dramatic deaths are separated by many years. That doesn't mean that the holiday is a profane occasion. Sacrificial deaths are sacred deaths, whether the victim is willing or not. Often, the deaths are sacrifices gone wrong.

Sacrifice, in its most basic terms, is giving something valuable to the gods or to a single deity. The main idea is that giving (hopefully) obligates some kind of reciprocity. It's basic human exchange practice writ large. There are any number of ways it can go wrong: a sacrifice isn't acceptable, for instance, or the will of the gods may have been misread. Perhaps the sacrifice isn't adequate to overcome some human foible that annoyed a god. Human stand-ins for deities are common.

While engaged in Christmas shopping, thoughts of sacrifice are perhaps far from the mind. Imagining the joy evoked or anticipating the delighted surprise from a present may be more common. Giving of our own resources for the happiness of another, however, is a form of sacrifice. The gremlin Gizmo, after all, is a gift. Deeper theological roots lie behind sacrifice, as will be explored in chapter 4. Most religious holidays involve some form of sacrifice. There may be feasting (the gods sharing slaughtered animals) or relaxation from work (giving up productive time)—sacrifice pervades holiday celebrations.

Not all holidays have religious origins, as noted. April Fool's Day (the holiday; also the title of Fred Walton's 1986 film) has unknown origins but there's really nothing religious at all about it. Still, it qualifies as holiday horror. Putting an outlier into the discussion helps to sharpen the focus on what distinguishes the sub-genre. Even in this secular holiday movie based on a secular holiday, sacrifice is involved. The reveal at the end exposes Muffy St. John's (Deborah Foreman) ruse, but along the way the first-time viewer has to suppose the deaths of her friends and staff are real. Again, this is a kind of sacrifice, although not a religious one.

Our current perspective on holidays tends to be lighthearted. The more somber days—Yom Kippur or Good Friday—tend to be non-commercialized and overlooked by the non-religious. Even Thanksgiving, which, for many, starts the American "holiday season," is commercialized by various food companies and is a day of horror for turkeys. After all, the next day is Black Friday, which, unlike Good Friday, is a day for spending and celebration. Thanksgiving hasn't escaped holiday horror, of course, but the focus on "turkey day" underscores once again the sacrificial aspect.

Apart from being liminal in the sense of outside ordinary time, holy days also inherently involve sacrifice. Whether figurative or literal, sacrifice is part of the picture. This plays into holiday horror as well; the sacred context of the holy day makes a mundane murder a sacrifice. This aspect will be examined more fully in chapter 4.

VACATION ON SUMMERISLE

Think about your work or school schedule. It is likely bookended by weekends and punctuated with various days off for one reason or another. There may be company or university holidays. And then there's vacation. All of this time off has its origins in sacred time.

Now think about our pre-agricultural ancestors. Like most other animals, if they didn't go out daily to procure food, to find the raw materials they needed for their homes, or other necessities, they wouldn't survive long. There were no regular days off. The earliest recorded special times—holy days—occur after agrarian life began. Societies organized around agriculture could achieve food surpluses which allowed for religiously sanctioned days when work was deemed inappropriate. The earliest recorded cultures with written annals recognized religious holidays. Otherwise labor was a daily task, with no weekends (Johnston, 2015: 121–23).

The elites of ancient societies could, and did, mark astronomical seasons—equinoxes and solstices—and even the average person could tell when days were longer or shorter, in any region apart from the tropics. Far more obvious to most were the changes in the moon. Not only were lunar phases visible, they were also quite predictable. Most ancient calendars were lunar and many festivals fell on certain phases of the moon. Since the moon was generally a deity, those holidays were religious occasions.

Weeks do not correspond to any regular changes in heavenly bodies like years or months do. The origin of the seven-day week appears to have begun with the Judaic observation of the Sabbath. This marked the eventual standard of a fixed number of working days in what would come to be known as the week.

Early Christians were Jews, and when Sunday—the day of resurrection—was added to the Sabbath (Saturday), the concept of a five-day work week began to evolve. This took many centuries, however; our modern idea of a two-day weekend only appeared in the 1930s. Prior to that it was common for industrial workers to have one day off in a week. Starting in the nineteenth century, business owners, in efforts to recruit workers, began to offer standard hours. Obviously this doesn't apply to all professions, but the idea of offering two consecutive days off included one for spending and one for worshipping. Or the other way around. Our modern weekend, which is pretty standard for most western societies and the only usual system in living memory, has only been around for the length of a single lifetime (Sopher, 2014). Its origin is ultimately religious, bolstered by business.

Even though there are many secular holidays, the holy-day concept is religious in origin. So is the concept of vacation. While historians haven't written a ton of books about the history of the concept, a few basic points are clear—traveling for leisure is a fairly new phenomenon, it requires some measure of affluence, and it began as a form of pilgrimage. Pilgrims, of course, travel to locations of religious significance. Even today, rest and relaxation is sometimes referred to as spiritual rejuvenation. The practice of spending time not working is based in religion.

With this added dimension we'll be able to see more clearly the liminal-time aspect of horror that focuses on time out of the ordinary. Holidays are the main examples of this, but the British use of "holiday" to encompass time spent away also plays into it. This can be seen as early as the *Canterbury Tales* and as recently as films like *The Evil Dead* (Sam Raimi, 1981), *Cabin Fever* (Eli Roth, 2002), or *The Cabin in the Woods* (Drew Goddard, 2011). *The Hills Have Eyes* (Wes Craven, 1977) could also qualify since the Carter family is on vacation, but in that case they never make it to their destination.

In *The Evil Dead* the young people read aloud ancient Sumerian curses that cause them to be attacked by demons. *Cabin Fever*, moving away from the religious origins, instead sees the outbreak of a flesh-eating virus getting in the way of a good time. *The Cabin in the Woods* posits that the entire holiday is a set-up to appease the old gods who, as in *Wicker Man*, require sacrifice. Expanding the narrow confines of holiday horror to include these kinds of films does no violence to the sub-genre. Instead of a bad history of the day, there's more of a bad history of the place. The anniversary of a killing is certainly present in *The Evil Dead* (consider all that creepy stuff in the basement, as well as the professor's own account of events) and *The Cabin in the Woods*. In the latter the date by which the old gods must be appeased with sacrifice is inviolable. All three of these films enter that liminal time that vacations share with holidays, and the results are similar.

CELTIC HOLIDAYS

Some holidays—those that have commercial potential like Halloween or Christmas—have quite a few books written about them. Other, lesser-celebrated holidays—May Day, for example—not so much. Accurate information on pre-Christian holidays, such as those of ancient Europe, is often difficult to track down. Modern revival religions—present-day celebrations of Imbolc or Beltane, for example—often involve reconstructions based on many sources, not all of them historically accurate. One of the reasons for this is that we don't know as much about ancient cultures that didn't leave treasure troves of written records.

Compare ancient Greece or Rome. We have libraries full of the classics, from Cicero to Suetonius, from Aristotle to Zeno. Indeed, the field of classics has its work cut out for it with an entire massive canon of ancient works. The Celts and the Anglo-Saxons, on the other hand, didn't leave behind huge libraries about their cultures (Chadwick, 1971: 46–53). We learn about the tradition of the wicker man, for example, from Julius Caesar (who is probably drawing from Posidonius; Ellis, 2002: 50), not from Celtic descriptions of their own rites. Outsiders, such as Caesar, both exaggerate and misinterpret, particularly when they're attempting to discredit.

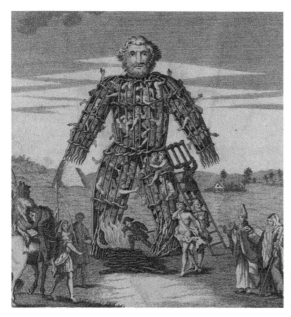

Figure 2. Fanciful wicker man from Thomas Pennant (1726–1798), A Tour in Wales. Public domain

Historians of ancient holidays, often providing the information in the context of ancient religions, reconstruct celebrations on the basis of three main sources: archaeological finds, more recent records that may describe older traditions, and careful use of outside sources such as Caesar and other classical writers. The results are patchy. A good example of this will be the Wheel of the Year, discussed in the next chapter, which includes Beltane, or May Day. This lack of solid information leaves plenty of room for holiday horror to explore.

These Celtic "pagan" holidays, being mysterious, allow for the fear of the unknown to add to the uncertainty Howie experiences in the movie. What these isolated people are doing is completely unfamiliar to him. His use of "pagan" against Lord Summerisle in their first interview is intended as a moral condemnation. A word about "pagan" and "heathen" will be helpful before getting to holiday horror proper, so that you don't have to keep seeing scare quotes.

PAGANISM

Religion is a funny thing. There was no word for religion before Christianity came along.[6] It was largely what folk believed or did. Of course, there were official, sometimes national, ritual practices. Scholars unhelpfully call these "cult practices." Cult here simply means the specific practice of religious rituals. In ancient times there was no separation between government and religion (no "church and state"). Religious institutions, largely outside the life of the average person, could either support or vie for authority against monarchies. Both were sources of tremendous wealth and power and neither particularly cared what the average person believed as long as they paid when they were taxed.

That began to change with the emergence of monotheism. With multiple gods, if one is offended you can appeal to another for help. But if there's only one deity and that deity is offended by the behavior of the folk, then everyone has a stake in keeping that god happy. This was the context into which Christianity was born. While its parent religion, Judaism, had rules and commandments, Christianity soon set itself against many of the accepted values of its world; this included other belief systems. In a way that was perhaps more intense than any other form of religious expression, Christianity emphasized the need for correct belief. Not only did an individual's salvation depend upon it, so did keeping God happy. And that implicated everyone.

Although early Christianity was never unified (the Catholic tradition won out in numbers, but there were alternate forms of Christianity from the beginning), it soon developed the characteristic of calling out those who believed differently. If the "wrong" belief was one that claimed to follow Christ, it was called heresy. If that belief fell outside the Christian tradition, it was "pagan." Pagan simply signified "not Christian," but it was used pejoratively. Those who believed differently were somehow less than Christians who followed what they perceived to be the only truth. Another word for pagan was "heathen"—"holding religious beliefs of a sort that are considered unenlightened, now esp. ones of a primitive or polytheistic nature; spec. not of the Christian, Jewish, or Muslim faiths," according to the *Oxford English Dictionary*. In other words, those who do not count themselves monotheistic are by definition heathen. *The Wicker Man* uses that dynamic conflict quite effectively, focusing it on May Day. *Midsommar*, produced some decades later, took a similar approach, using secular protagonists on a different holiday.

As utilized in this book the terms pagan and heathen are used more or less interchangeably and without disparagement. Scholars of religion recognize that folk religions—sometimes called animism or shamanism—are a legitimate expression of human religious sentiment. Even that statement demonstrates how deeply rooted Christianity remains in our culture: what right have scholars of religion (in a system established in a Christian context) to recognize a religion as legitimate or not?[7]

Since western culture has been dominated by various forms of Christianity for centuries, both "pagan" and "heathen" came to denote debased, degenerate individuals who stubbornly refused to acknowledge the "one true religion." In the study of religion in more recent times, pagan is used as a neutral term while heathen has been largely discarded.

Scholars of religion have come to take a kindlier view of these non-Christian forms of religion over the past several decades. We don't always have extensive written records about them. (In spite of the problems it has caused, Christianity was largely responsible for promoting literacy.) Indigenous religions don't really fall into a single belief structure. While today "pagan" can be used as a badge of honor, in the 1970s it was still a slur.

The Wicker Man sets itself in the world of reconstructed pre-Christian Celtic religion. In this it shares a remote ancestor with *Halloween*, which followed five years later. *Wicker Man* is set on May Day, and the eponymous title for what the Celts called Samhain (Halloween) occurred half a year later, in October.[8] The Celts recognized four major seasonal holidays, to be discussed in the next chapter. Remember, *Halloween* wasn't the first holiday horror movie, but it was the film that brought the concept to popular awareness. Five years earlier *The Wicker Man* used another Celtic holiday to comment on belief. It was making a point about religions, but not necessarily only pagan ones.

A CAUTIONARY TALE

We've briefly looked at David Pinner's novel *Ritual* in the introduction. A novelist, of course, doesn't fix the meaning of a movie.[9] Commercial films are never an individual effort. Just consider the lengthy credits on most modern movies—and even those can't cover everyone involved. It's shorthand to consider the director and screenwriter, Robin

Hardy and Anthony Shaffer in this case, as the ones who determine what a film means. In reality it's a much more subtle interplay between them, the actors, the editor, and many others. Finally, the viewer also determines what a film means for her- or himself.

Having said that, the director's vision and the screenwriter's script are important components for the message of a movie. The documentary *The Wicker Man Enigma* includes interviews with many of the cast and crew. In his first appearance Robin Hardy notes that the movie is a cautionary tale. On the surface it might seem that he intended to warn of the dangers of pagan religion,[10] but this caution bears further consideration. It's no longer possible to ask Hardy what exactly he meant; we must probe the film directly.[11]

Throughout Sgt. Howie's tenure on Summerisle, he's shown as completely intolerant to the religion of the friendly, mostly polite, citizens of the island. They don't lose their tempers as he bursts into their houses frantically searching for Rowan. When he walks in on the librarian taking a bath, she doesn't even scream. Yes, they murder him at the end, but their daily existence, apart from the plot, seems almost idyllic. But the religion of Summerisle isn't Christian. It isn't immoral either (Ingham, 2018: 36–42, opines differently).

What exactly Hardy meant by a cautionary tale died with him, but given subsequent political developments tied closely to the evangelical strains of Christianity, a caution against taking any religion to extremes seems to match his worries. Believers who go too far aren't limited to paganism. Indeed, the fuel for many holidays that are considered civil and even Christian can lead to fatal consequences, as holiday horror suggests. Tragic stampedes at religious gatherings are occasional news items. Even the Christian commercial backing of Christmas is a component of a larger system that oppresses many, even to the point of shortening their lives. Religion participates in what Douglas Cowan (2020) calls the "good, moral, and decent fallacy." Just because it's religious doesn't mean it's good.

In *The Wicker Man* two religions that are unwilling to bend collide over a holiday. It's an intentional meeting—no one is allowed on Summerisle without the laird's permission—but Howie's religion also brooks no competition. "And what of the true God? Whose glory, churches and monasteries have been built on these islands for generations past?

Now sir, what of him?" he challenges Lord Summerisle. Other religions are fine as long as everyone acknowledges that only Christianity is the correct one.

Interestingly, May Day is one of the few pre-Christian holidays that the church made no real efforts to supplant. Perhaps since Easter is a moveable feast (one whose date is not fixed, generally because it's based on a lunar calendar) and can fall as late as April 25, there was not much need for Christianizing Beltane.[12] The holiday, in *The Wicker Man*, is the occasion for a human sacrifice, like Easter—on at least a theological level. Before becoming judgmental, it's important to realize that Christianity is also based on the concept of human sacrifice. Jesus' death is still referred to in the Anglican mass, Howie's own religion, as a sacrifice. As we'll see shortly, however, human sacrifice was not a known historical feature of Beltane.

Caution here warns against taking any religion too seriously. Religion itself can be problematic. Apart from the violence they frequently spawn, religions are a financial commitment. Most of the time you can't join without making some kind of financial pledge. Religion within capitalism must raise money. True believers are often unaware of this economic component of their belief systems. Taking the stories to be facts, they get carried away with obeying to the letter while leaders are interested in turning a profit. That's as true of bishops on the mainland as it is of Lord Summerisle.

Although in present times we're used to "Nones" and there's little social stigma to not being religious, that was not yet the case in the early 1970s. A deep distrust of those who believed differently pervaded much of western culture. Fear of "cults" was widespread. Just two decades later widespread Satanic panic gripped much of the western world, even though evidence of any pervasive Satanism was lacking (Ellis, 2000: 3). It seems likely that Anthony Shaffer was knowingly nodding his head.

FLASHBACKS

Sergeant Howie's religion is shown, apart from through the dialogue in which he engages, via a series of flashbacks during his fateful first night on Summerisle.[13] He's already been considerably primed by the islanders during the day. They all deny recognizing Rowan Morrison (Geraldine Cowper) when he shows her photograph around. When he finally gets them to admit to having Morrisons on the island, Rowan's own mother denies that Rowan is her daughter. In fact, her nine-year-old daughter Myrtle (Jennifer Martin) tells Sgt. Howie that Rowan's a hare. His inquiry leading nowhere, he heads to the Green Man, to find the locals drinking and carousing on a Sunday night.[14]

That night his room at the inn is one thin door away from that of Willow, the landlord's daughter. Howie is on his knees in prayer next to his bed. An urging song starts up and Willow, naked, dances through her room, asking him to come over. The flashbacks occur in this scene of temptation. First we see Howie in an Anglican church, reading the Epistle lesson (a priest or deacon reads the Gospel lesson).[15] The reading is from Paul's first letter to the Corinthians (11.23–26), about the establishment of the Lord's Supper—a Christian springtime observance, tying May Day into Easter. The holidays are brought into contrast here.

This sequence of flashback shots establishes the religion of Sgt. Howie. More than that, it also sets up the central conflict of the plot—traditional Christianity versus any comers. Since the nineteenth century there have been more Catholics than Anglicans in Scotland (Lynch, 1991). Both Anglican and Catholic would object to what Willow is proposing. Clearly Howie's not a member of the Church of Scotland, which is Presbyterian. Although Robin Hardy had his reasons for this (Franks et al., 2007), Calvinism might have arguably been a better choice for a Scot.

Apart from being less dramatic in worship, Presbyterianism is a relatively recent form of Christianity. It does, however, hold very strict behavioral codes as it lacks confession as a sacrament (Howie doesn't want to die unshriven). The significance of religion in the history of the British Isles is nevertheless clear. Remember, from the time of Henry VIII onward, the religion of the monarch was the religion of the realm. This had serious consequences during the Tudor period and later, when your personal religion could be a cause of death if it differed from the religion of the crown. *The Wicker Man* is a cautionary tale in more than one way. Howie ignores the violent history of his own religion within Britain.

Something both Anglicanism and Catholicism share is their tradition of continuity with the very first Christians. Although the rituals evolved over time, the teaching for each is still that the basics behind the mass were handed down from the very beginning of Christian worship. The tradition, according to doctrine, stretches all the way back to St. Peter. Not only that, but the Eucharist, which Howie is shown receiving, is considered essential for the unity of the tradition. It is a visible sign of belonging. On Summerisle, all of that is gone. The indigenous religion recognizing the old gods claims to be more ancient, more in keeping with the land itself.

Sergeant Howie, Bible-reading, communion-partaking, praying at the bedside, is fully invested in a supersessionist Christianity—the belief that Christianity supersedes all other previous religions. The paganism of Summerisle pushes back. Each claims an ancient pedigree. Being folk horror, however, the landscape will help decide the winner, and Howie is most definitely walking on pagan bedrock.

Willow's dance scene, with its celebration of sexuality conflicting with a cheerless religion of self-restraint and decorum, leads to a dark night of the soul for Howie. His religion has demonized sexuality from at least the time of Augustine of Hippo in the fourth and fifth centuries (see Endsjø, 2011, discussed below in chapter 3). His response is, of course, a test. The sexual frustration, demonstrated the next morning as Willow wakens Howie, firmly rests in his Christian understanding of sexuality (see chapter 3).[16] Without knowing it, no matter what Howie does he will be condemned either by his own faith or in the celebration of a pagan holiday. May Day on Summerisle is a joyous occasion. The "Christian copper," however, isn't in a party mood.

Figure 3. Howie's bras d'honneur. © *British Lion*

RELIGION-HORROR

This religion-horror mix isn't uncommon for post-1968 horror films. Just as *The Wicker Man* is part of the "unholy trinity" of folk horror, another unholy trinity of strongly Christian-themed horror began in 1968 with Roman Polanski's *Rosemary's Baby*. The central premise, that the Devil has raped Rosemary and she is bearing his son, is clearly based on Christian concepts; the Devil grew out of Christianity. An inversion of the Christmas story where Mary bears the son of God, *Rosemary's Baby* shocked, scandalized, and frightened audiences just before the dawn of the seventies.

The second "person" of this religious trinity was William Friedkin's *The Exorcist*, released the same year as *The Wicker Man*. Perhaps the most theologically aware horror film ever, this movie almost singlehandedly revived modern interest in demons and kickstarted the present-day demand for exorcisms. It also demonstrated that horror based on religious concepts could be wildly successful. And taken literally.

The Omen (Richard Donner, 1976), just three years later, is the third of this unholy triad. It introduced the Antichrist as a horror figure, even before *Left Behind*. Although the general public might believe the Bible has a consistent Antichrist character, that's not really the case. He's as fabricated as Summerisle's May Day. Together these three movies paved the way for other horror that takes its energy from religious themes, and the flow of religion-based horror hasn't slowed yet (Wiggins, 2018).

Christianity drives *The Wicker Man* as well, although the movie is about its clash with reimagined Celtic religion. It's important to remember that this is a cautionary tale about taking religion too seriously. That religion could well be Christianity. While Robin Hardy may have been truly concerned about isolated pagans in the Scottish isles, it makes sense to see the fear applying to any religion, especially for a religion that has a history of martyr complexes and many days in its calendars that celebrate the deaths—often cruel and unusual—of its saints. But how does Christianity drive *The Wicker Man*?

First of all, it sets up the conflict. A bunch of pagan Scots on an island doesn't bother anyone. When they need an outside sacrifice—they don't commit murder, as Lord Summerisle declares, being a highly moral people—they need to victimize another religion. In Britain of the 1970s Christianity was the majority religion.

The sacrifice requires a special occasion, and here again Christianity tolerates no rival celebrations, taking over significant dates. The occasion is May Day, when the crops are being planted and the trees are blossoming. Perhaps they're not well remembered these days, but the old British Christian observation of rogation days challenges the pagan May Day. Rogation days are when priests would bless the fields before planting. A practice believed to have originated in eighth-century England, rogation days were church-sanctioned occasions to ensure a good harvest. Fully vested in liturgical haberdashery, the priest would lead a congregation, chanting the Litany of the Saints, out to a farm field where he would bless it with holy water. Sounds almost pagan, doesn't it? Occurring on April 25 the major rogation day stands less than a week from May Day. Rogation days, however, never became major holidays.

Quite a bit of running time for *The Wicker Man* involves Summerisle's explanation of how the old religion began due to agricultural necessity. Among the most beloved of British Christian hymns is "We Plough the Fields and Scatter."[17] Although a harvest hymn, the first stanza makes it clear that the Christian God is responsible for the bounty:

> We plough the fields, and scatter the good seed on the land;
> But it is fed and watered by God's almighty hand:
> He sends the snow in winter, the warmth to swell the grain,
> The breezes and the sunshine, and soft refreshing rain.[18]

Without the assurance that it is the Christian deity who is responsible for crops—remember Howie's desperate plea just before he's carried to the wicker man—there's no reason to dispute paganism. The growth of crops is natural. So are blight and drought. Different religions, however, explain this in conflicting ways. No matter what your religion is, gods decide on whether to reward humans with sufficient crops or not. Religions have traditionally celebrated the cycle of the year with holidays. Before becoming theologized by Christianity, they were opportunities to encourage the progress of nature. Ignoring that could lead to consequences. Dire consequences.

IS SACRIFICE MURDER?

Remember, Anthony Shaffer stated plainly that *The Wicker Man* was about sacrifice.

Sacrifice is always disturbing and has to be accompanied by true belief to be effective. Lord Summerisle explains to Howie that his grandfather bought the island in 1868 to carry out his agrarian experiments. His portrait depicts him wearing a black frock and carrying a large book as he glares down on his work. The painting is almost a pagan icon.

The fertile volcanic soil and warmth of the Gulf Stream suggested that if he could motivate the dispirited denizens, he would make the place fruitful again. "So, with typical mid-Victorian zeal, he set to work. The best way of accomplishing this, so it seemed to him, was to rouse the people from their apathy by giving them back their joyous old gods, and it is as a result of this worship the barren island would burgeon and bring forth fruit in great abundance," Lord Summerisle explains. Giving back the old gods implies that they had been taken away by Christianity. This led to the islanders' lack of enthusiasm for trying to scratch a living from the rocky soil. The plan worked. Summerisle explains that after the hardier strains developed by his grandfather began to bear fruit, the Christian clergy fled. This point is in its own way an intimation of sacrifice. To become pagan, the Christian clergy had to be "sacrificed."

"What my grandfather had started out of expediency, my father continued out of love. He brought me up the same way, to reverence the music and the drama and the rituals of the old gods. To love nature and to fear it. And to rely on it and to appease it where necessary," Summerisle explains. Among the parts cut from the theatrical version is a lengthier explanation of the theology at play here, unfortunately lost (Bartholomew, 1977: 38).[19] This theology will be our concern in chapter 4. At this point the essential aspect is that the islanders became believers. For believers, sacrifice isn't murder.

Lest Howie object, which he does, it could be pointed out that he came to the island of his own free will. Yes, he was lied to, but a sacrifice has to be volitional. Had he stayed away he would've saved his life. Coming to Summerisle, in the eyes of their gods, is an act of willingness. To come to the island at May Day is to be subject to the rules of May Day.

Although Robin Hardy claimed the wicker man is well attested, historically it comes down to one line by Julius Caesar that isn't connected with May Day. Commenting on the Celts, Caesar wrote, "Others have figures of vast size, the limbs of which formed of osiers they fill with living men, which being set on fire, the men perish enveloped in the flames" (Caesar, *The Gallic War*. book VI, chapter XVI). He is discussing—largely at second hand—the sacrificial beliefs among the Gauls (ancient Celts). Evidence for widespread human sacrifice in ancient Europe is lacking; it took place only on occasion, as noted above. Indeed, part of what would make it so effective would be the shocking nature of the act. That also works for *The Wicker Man*. Historically there are many problems with Caesar's claim, not least the structural and economic aspects of using such an elaborate form of public execution (Hutton, 2011: 3, 70). Nevertheless, the logic he uses—that the sacrifice is to please the gods for national purposes—fits nicely into the diegesis of the film. As Lord Summerisle says, "Animals are fine, but their acceptability is limited. A little child is even better, but not nearly as effective as the right kind of adult."

This brings us back to sacrifice, Shaffer's point in the screenplay. This is also an underlying theme in Pinner's novel; the ending, however, calls this into question. Historically, archaeology and literature concur that Celts did practice some human sacrifice (Hutton, 2011: 25; Green, 2011: 25–28). For them it wasn't murder. May Morrison (Irene Sunter) puts it best. On the frantic morning of May Day, she says to Howie, "You'll simply never understand the true nature of sacrifice."

MARTYRDOM

Sacrifice and martyrdom are not the same thing, but they are closely related. The concept of sacrifice runs deeply in religious thought and is essential to many holidays, as chapter 4 will explore. In Christianity, from Christmas to Easter the story of Jesus is one long preparation for his sacrifice. Jewish holidays, as described in the Bible, frequently involve a special sacrifice. In Christianity sacrifice became the central theme. All non-Christian sacrifice was literally demonized.

After Jesus' death, however, some of his followers went unwillingly (or sometimes too willingly) to their deaths because of their beliefs. "Martyr" translates as "witness," and it was the term used by those Christians who provoked the Roman authorities to put them to death. For some time young Christianity was illegal in the Roman Empire. Christians who were caught could be punished by death. Most of them, it seems, weren't trying to get themselves killed (although some were). Believing their deaths to be a kind of sacrifice, they had the afterlife to anticipate. These martyrs believed their deaths were witness to the truth of their beliefs about Jesus.

The Wicker Man is aware of this subtlety. Just prior to being locked in the wicker man, Sgt. Howie disputes with Lord Summerisle and the islanders about, interestingly enough, theology. We'll look at this in more detail in chapter 4, but the idea ties into the May Day sacrifice that gives the movie its power. Howie loudly proclaims that he is a Christian and doesn't believe in their gods or their rituals. He declares that he believes he will receive everlasting life for observing his faith—the only true religion.

From the perspective of the pagans Howie will be an acceptable, willing sacrifice to Nuada and Avellenau. From Howie's perspective he is certainly not willing. Understanding that perspective, Summerisle can see that Howie's death becomes, in his own eyes, a martyrdom. This is some fine theological thinking for a horror movie.

Much of the Christian holiday calendar consists of death dates of martyrs. Even at this point, horror stands behind the holidays. None of this would happen, however, without the tradition of sacrifice on a major religious holiday. Without May Day there would be no *Wicker Man*.

NOTES

1. Carpenter would, of course, go on to direct a remake of *The Thing from Another World*, known as *The Thing*, in 1982.
2. See the interview with Robin Hardy in Franks et al. (2007) and Christopher Lee's recollections presented in Brown (2000).
3. The concern with fertility in *Midsommar* is *human* reproduction, something Robin Hardy also explored in *The Wicker Tree* (2011).
4. As made clear in Kier-La Janisse's 2021 documentary *Woodlands Dark and Days Bewitched: A History of Folk Horror*.
5. *A History of Horror with Mark Gatiss*, part 2, "Home Counties Horror" (2010).
6. See, for example, Smith (1991: 15–22). Ancient peoples had religious behaviors, but no word that equates to "religion."
7. In civil cases it is frequently a matter of tax exemption that forces government officials to determine if a religion is legitimate. Different tax laws apply, and once money gets involved all bets are off.
8. Precise dating becomes confused with the changing of calendars from Julian to Gregorian, as well as the tendency for ancient festivals to fall on a range of days. Even today, Christian

observance of All Hallows' Eve depends on All Saints' Day (November 1) and All Souls' Day (November 2), forming a sequence of holy days.

9.   Robin Hardy and Anthony Shaffer later novelized the movie in *The Wicker Man* (1978).

10. Hardy and Shaffer were wary of the New Age movement; see the Introduction of Franks et al. (2006). Hardy apparently intended caution concerning reemerging paganism. Shaffer's comments in Bartholomew (1977: 16) leave more ambiguity on his point of view.

11. It is tempting to bring Hardy's *The Wicker Tree* into the discussion as it shows a less-than-flattering Christianity, but our focus here is what *The Wicker Man* itself suggests.

12. The date of Easter is determined by this formula: Easter is the first Sunday after the first full moon after the vernal equinox. If the full moon falls on the equinox on Saturday March 21, Easter is at its earliest: March 22. If the full moon falls on that Sunday, another month is required for it to cycle back, giving Easter a date late in April. (Orthodox Christianity follows the Julian calendar but uses the same formula.)

13. The timing of the director's cut is different; there are no flashbacks because this scene takes place before Howie ever came to Summerisle, and Willow's invitation to Howie takes place on his second night at the Green Man.

14. Again, the longer version sets up a different timing; this is one reason that the year the movie is set is important. Obviously, as originally set in the director's cut, Howie would've arrived on a different day. Since the children are in school the next morning, however, this fits with the timing of May Day 1973.

15. Robin Hardy confirms (as well as details of the ritual) that Howie is Anglican. See the interviews with Hardy in Franks et al. (2007) and Paciorek et al. (2018: 369). The novelization affirms this.

16. The hard, trembling gesture Howie makes with his hand as he tightens his watchband mirrors precisely that of the baker (John MacGregor) performing a *bras d'honneur* during the singing of "The Landlord's Daughter" the night before.

17. https://www.telegraph.co.uk/news/uknews/1486529/Traditional-songs-beat-the-happy-clappers-hands-down-in-search-for-Britains-best-hymns.html.

18. Jane Montgomery Campbell translation, 1861, available in many Christian hymnals. The hymn text was originally written in German by Matthias Claudius.

19. The dialogue is preserved in Scene 85 of Shaffer's script.

CHAPTER 2: MAY DAY

Nearly unnoticed, as Sgt. Howie pulls out Miss Rose's classroom register to look up Rowan Morrison, the camera skims the top of the page where the words "Belthane Term" appear. The school, in keeping with old English practice, divides the terms based on their major holidays.[1] *The Wicker Man* almost exclusively prefers May Day for the name of the holiday; Beltane and its variants are the more usual Gaelic titles in modern paganism.

Figure 4. The only Belthane in the movie. © British Lion

Almost immediately for the holiday history we run into a problem. Written records, which are necessary to construct accurate histories, are lacking for much of ancient Celtic culture. Druids, the intellectual class of the Celts, forbade the writing of their teachings (Ellis, 2002: 14). As noted in the last chapter, even our knowledge of the wicker man, if there ever actually was such a thing, comes from the Roman reflections of Julius Caesar. Literacy was fairly rare in antiquity and often reserved for the elites. Although some ancient historians thought to preserve the reasons behind their holidays, knowledge of such things was generally presumed. Holidays were celebrated and people knew why. This hardly seemed to require special, written explanation. The end result of all of this is that those who try to piece together ancient holidays and celebrations have to draw from many sources, some of them historically suspect.

The Celts seem to have had four major holidays at the start of the seasons, not necessarily as measured by the solstices and equinoxes, but in response to levels of light and warmth. Their major holidays were Samhain, Imbolc, Beltane, and Lughnasadh;

of these, Samhain, which evolved into Halloween, is the most famous. They will be considered in more detail under the Wheel of the Year. While historians such as Ronald Hutton (1991, 1996) do their best to dig out information on pre-Christian holidays, quite a lot is left to speculation. One reason for this was the conquest of pagan religions by Christianity.

So successful was the Christianization of the British Isles that it is doubtful that any of the old religions survived continuously. They never disappeared completely, but they retained no unbroken tradition reaching back to antiquity. As is often the case when older forms of religion are rediscovered, modern revivals of those religions take place. There are thriving cultures of revival religions surrounding Norse mythology, Greek mythology, and even Canaanite mythology. Since none of these survived intact, the modern revivals have to reconstruct what might've been done or believed.

The summary in this chapter is very simplified, and I will be using Wicca as a guide since it is the largest and most widely recognized of revival earth-centered, or nature-based, religions. There are also what are called Celtic Reconstructionist religions (NicDhàna et al., 2007). Unlike Christianity these religions have no single leader who determines the correct way that the theology of the calendar works out. Instead, these various belief systems draw their inspiration from some twentieth-century experimenters who brought these ideas to modern awareness.

Earth-centered religions, such as Wicca, have redeveloped the ancient Celtic holidays. There are different kinds of Wicca, but the modern religion developed initially out of the work of Gerald Gardner (1884–1964) in England. Gardner was a civil servant who was largely responsible for reigniting interest in witchcraft. Assuming the work of Margaret Murray (1863–1963)—an academic historian and folklorist—was accurately describing the continuation of the witch cult in Europe, he set about reconstructing that witchcraft (Russell and Alexander, 2007: 158–62). Murray was an Egyptologist by training, but her ideas about the European witch cult were wide-reaching, rather like Frazer's *Golden Bough*. She claimed that some pockets of this old religion had survived, and it seems likely that Gardner believed that to be the case. Murray's hypothesis has since been largely discredited (Hutton, 1999: 194–201; Krzywinska, 2000: 78).

Gardner, however, was also influenced by Aleister Crowley (1875–1947), the famed English occultist and founder of Thelema (Russell and Alexander, 2007: 158). Crowley was no historian but instead relied heavily on esoterica. Gardner used Crowley's and Murray's work to help reconstruct what he believed was the old religion of Europe. Wicca grew out of, and diversified from, Gardner's efforts to reinstate Europe's pre-Christian religion. Elements of this that originated in David Pinner's *Ritual* remain in *The Wicker Man*. For example, Pinner's Hanlin is convinced of the reality of, and wants to root out, witches. The villagers control his mind at times (although that may be a delusion). In the film Lord Summerisle tells Sgt. Howie that they have controlled his every thought since he landed on the island. In the novel the villagers literally get into Hanlin's head; on Summerisle they simply leave intriguing clues. The suggested paganism has little of Gardnerian witchcraft in it, but it does borrow some ideas about the appropriate time for sacrifices.

Wicca, as a largely English movement to start with, grew from Gardner's open advocacy of this kind of nature religion. One of the developments from all of this was the "Wheel of the Year" (Bellenir, 2004: 265). This wheel has eight spokes that mark the progression of the seasons—they are festivals, or sabbats, that fall on or near the solstices and equinoxes and the four holidays that fall roughly halfway between those points, the "cross-quarter" days. The ancient Celts venerated the four "cross-quarter" days, but seem not to have focused on solstices and equinoxes. The eight-spoked Wheel of the Year is a more recent invention. To understand *The Wicker Man*'s May Day, we need to spin that wheel.

THE WHEEL OF THE YEAR

A necessary preamble concerning time: holidays of any description are a reflection of liminal time. Liminal, or "between," time always holds potential danger. Things aren't business as usual. Horror quite often does this in terms of place. For example, folk horror, in which *Wicker Man* also participates, tends to isolate victims in a rural location. *Alien* (Ridley Scott, 1979) put the crew of the Nostromo in space, far, far from any help. *The Shining* (Stanley Kubrick, 1980) put the Torrance family in a mountain hotel cut off by snow. Horror makes good use of liminal space.

Time can function in a similar way. At particular times the unexpected may happen. Holiday horror moves this beyond simple bad timing. There are occasions—red-letter days—that have a history, and that history leads to danger. Not only red-letter days, as we've seen, but time set apart from quotidian pursuits. While Christmas is the most popular holiday for horror, movies tied in with folk horror, such as *Wicker Man* and *Midsommar*, cash in on the unfamiliarity of a particular holiday. Everyone's seen a maypole, but who knows what really goes on with it? Modern-day people don't know the old, often isolated rites.

When a new year starts is really a matter of social preference. Today western culture tends to observe New Year on the first of January, but up until modern times it was often observed at the vernal equinox, the start of spring. Calendars can be confusing things because the year doesn't divide neatly into days. Because of this a number of methods have been utilized to keep the seasons aligned with calendar dates. If the actual solar year is about a quarter of a day longer than the days we divide by 24 hours, then about every four years there will be an extra day. Our current corrective is known as a leap year, and that keeps us roughly in line. The main concern is to keep the seasons aligned with the months we expect. Months, of course, marked the progress of the moon, but the tampering with months over time means they don't synchronize. Lunar phases require 29.5 days to cycle through, again not even with our convenient month lengths (Rothery, 2015: 46).

In societies that seem not to have had such strict adherence to the fiction of the modern calendar, there were other astronomical markers that a season was progressing. Those astronomical signals (solstices and equinoxes) didn't always map to when noticeable changes in the seasons actually began to appear. Keep in mind that what Summerisle explained to Howie is true: the Gulf Stream, which circulates warm water from near the equator all the way up to the British Isles, does affect the climate. Noticeable signs of spring, for example, may come in February, what many people think of as the dead of winter. Indeed, the meteorological seasons, as opposed to the astronomical ones, consider December, January, and February to be winter. Astronomically, winter continues until two-thirds of March is over.

Ancient peoples marked the solstices and equinoxes, but they lived closely to the land and considered signs, such as ewes lambing, as indications that spring was beginning as early as what we would call February 1. People in ancient times had many different new years, but it makes sense to begin exploring the Wheel of the Year with the winter solstice and its festival. In modern western culture it tends to be the biggest holiday of the year.

Throughout the northern hemisphere, celebrations of the growing of the light after the shortest day have long taken place (Aveny, 2003: 149–63). We know that even the Romans with their Mediterranean climate marked the season with festivals. At the time of the Roman Empire, the homeland of the Celts included eastern Europe. As Rome expanded, the Celts were pushed to the fringes of Roman control—Ireland, Scotland, the Isle of Man, Wales, and Brittany in northern France. Wicca tends to identify with the Celtic culture and calendar. Although we have little information about the Celtic winter solstice, it's convenient to borrow Yule as the title for the celebration.[2]

Yule is a Germanic holiday, and the various Germanic tribes were ancient northern neighbors to the Celts. It has become one of the eight sabbats of neo-paganism (and Wicca). Not much needs to be said about it here other than that some familiar Christmas traditions, such as Christmas trees, owe their origins to pagan celebrations of Yule.

Moving ahead in the year the next sabbat is Imbolc, on February 1. As I noted above, ewes begin lambing about that time of year, and this was apparently seen as the start of spring. It seems to have been a holiday to celebrate the goddess Brigit, later St. Brigit. Elements of Groundhog Day, again from Germanic lore, also play into the season that Christians restyled as Candlemas.

The vernal, or spring, equinox falls about two-thirds of the way through March, as noted. This sabbat is celebrated as Ostara, the goddess to whom it is dedicated (Kelly, 2017). The similarity of her name to Easter is not accidental. Easter is a moveable feast and is not reliably near the equinox. Since flowers start to bloom and rabbits start to emerge in profusion, this became a celebration of mid-spring, following on from Imbolc.

Beltane, or May Day, comes next. This will be described in some detail below.

Midsummer, brought back to popular consciousness by Ari Aster's *Midsommar*, is the sabbat on the longest day of the year, the summer solstice. Often celebrated with fire and divination, it was considered a time open to supernatural influences. It is also known by the title Litha in Wicca (Kelly, 2017). Given capitalism's slightly relaxed status regarding summer, this holiday has never been a major event in contemporary culture, although Christians had established it as St. John's Day instead of pagan Midsummer. Summer, due to the cycles of farm work, traditionally had many holidays (Homans, 1970: 366), the inverse of the present time.

Like Midsummer, Lughnasadh fell between the cracks with modern vacation times frequently timed in summer. Dedicated to the god Lugh, a very influential and widespread deity in Europe, this sabbat, which falls on August 1, was the beginning of autumn. Early harvesting soon starts.

Ironically, we hear little of the autumnal equinox in September apart from nights now being longer than days. There is no real holiday in the Christian calendar to correspond to it. It is known in neo-paganism as the sabbat of Mabon (Kelly, 2017).

Perhaps the most famous sabbat is Samhain. Horror fans are no strangers to Halloween, which is Christianity's answer to this holiday. Samhain occurs on November 1, the date to which the church transferred All Saints' Day, also known as All Hallows. The day before, October 31, was therefore All Hallows' Eve, which gives us our word Halloween. The modern traditions that mark the holiday largely come from Samhain, which was the Celtic new year.

The Wheel of the Year then spins back to Yule. We know very little about some of these days, historically. Even without many written records we can say that at least some of them were major holidays, and the cross-quarter days were certainly recognized among the Celts. And among those that had some survival into modern times was Beltane, or May Day.

Before we explore May Day and its representation in *The Wicker Man*, it's important to note that many of the pagan holidays for which we have evidence were celebrated with similar kinds of elements. Fire, for example, was essential to Yule, Imbolc, Beltane, Midsummer (Litha), and Samhain. No single holiday could be called *the* fire celebration.

Maypoles were sometimes used for Midsummer celebrations and not just for May Day. The holidays, in other words, were set markers in the turning of the year, but their celebrations held many features in common. *The Wicker Man* makes one holiday distinctive in its association with sacrifice.

MAY DAY ON SUMMERISLE

One of the Vander Kaays' qualifications for holiday horror is a bad association with the day. While *The Wicker Man* isn't titled after May Day, the holiday clearly dominates the movie.[3] Pinner's *Ritual*, as mentioned, had Midsummer as its pagan holiday. The ending of the novel leaves open to question what the natives of Thorn really do to celebrate Litha, but the holiday is obviously the breaking point for Detective Hanlin. In *The Wicker Man* May Day looms larger. In the diegesis of the film, this is the date for sacrifice to Nuada and Avellenau. How does this translate to a bad association?

If Howie has been drawn to the island as a sacrifice, it is implied that, whether or not this has happened before, May Day has the potential for its most solemn sacrifice—a human being. The day, in other words, is one of potential danger. The "deeply religious" islanders lured Howie to them specifically for this occasion. Killing him any other time would be murder.

Figure 5. Human cake. © *British Lion*

The first several scenes involve establishing shots to give the viewer an idea of Summerisle. What is this isolated location and how do the people behave? It's pretty disconcerting from the beginning. People open their windows and doors to stare at the stranger. Their customs are odd, as Howie can tell by even a glance at May Morrison's display of May Day sweets. Cakes shaped like babies (sugar babies in the novel) suggest something uncomfortable—the death and consumption of human beings. And people making love out in public? All of this demonstrates unfamiliar ways of thinking, and therefore uncertainty of motivation. And danger. The viewer is unsettled from the beginning. May Day is first mentioned the next morning.

The story unfolds over three days, with May Day being the culmination. Howie's first night tests his virginity and leads to the initial mention of the holiday in the next morning's conversation with Willow. As a Christian, Howie is likely unaware of any significance associated with the day. A few quaint May Day customs persist here and there, but it's not a major holiday. Easter, the defining Christian holiday, fell on April 22 in 1973. Christian teaching seldom bothers to explain other religions' holidays. Willow, upon waking Howie, advises him to leave that day. She's not sincere, of course, but it tests his willingness to stay.

Indeed, Howie remains, as anticipated, to investigate. Holidays in pre-modern times often spanned more than a single day. The most obvious example of this is Christmas, or Yule. Admittedly, agriculture is more relaxed in winter, but the various December holidays in Roman and other cultures stretched over periods of days. There's a remnant of this in the twelve days of Christmas. Other ancient festivals also lasted beyond a single day. The preparations for May Day are evident as Howie visits Rowan Morrison's school. Before he even reaches the girls' classroom, he encounters the Schoolmaster (Walter Carr) leading the boys in a maypole dance.[4] The clear phallic interpretation of the pole offends the policeman, and he walks into the trap set by the obviously empty desk in Miss Rose's (Diane Cilento) classroom. That empty desk, with its beetle going around the nail, although lost on Howie, foreshadows his fate. It also mirrors the maypole outside. We'll come back to the maypole shortly.

There's a festal air in the classroom as the girls beat out the rhythm to the song. They gleefully respond to their teacher's question. The lightness of the occasion anticipates the holiday. May 1 in 1973 was a Tuesday and, as Howie's second morning clearly reveals, a day off from work and school.[5] The day before the holiday, May Eve, was celebrated as Walpurgis Night in Germany, as May 1 was designed St. Walpurga's Day. Not a major figure, St. Walpurga was known in Germanic tradition as protecting folk from witchcraft. This becomes significant in the use nature religions make of Celtic holidays. Apart from the *Night on Bald Mountain* (Modest Mussorgsky and Nikolay Rimsky-Korsakov) giving kids nightmares thanks to Disney's *Fantasia* (1940), it also reflects the association of the day before May Day. The day Howie visits the school would be Monday, May Eve.

The remainder of May Eve is spent in investigation. On his way to Lord Summerisle's castle, Howie witnesses the young girls dancing naked around a bonfire in a stone circle that resembles a small Stonehenge. This too is preparation for May Day. So is the blessing of the apple blossoms by pregnant women.

May Day itself is a blend of frantic searching for Rowan and the community's apparently unconcerned festal atmosphere. The trio of the hobbyhorse, the man-woman teaser, and the fool are preparing for their roles as other, somewhat sinister, preparations are made (boiling tar in a large caldron, for example, while not explicit, suggests burning without actually showing it). The hobbyhorse, teaser, and fool, as we'll see in the next section, have actual associations with May Day, but not necessarily together. Once the procession begins we're introduced to the sword dancers. Unnamed, they have the role of ritual executioners in the rite at the stone circle. Of course, it's not the game of chance Lord Summerisle claims it to be, for the May Queen, a girl named Holly (Fiona Kennedy), is the victim, although it's only her artificial hare's head that's severed.[6]

The offering of ale to the god of the sea is the prelude to human sacrifice. This god isn't named, and since the Celtic gods' names don't always correspond to known deities in the *Wicker Man* diegesis, we can only speculate who it is. The final rite involves the reveal. Howie is shown Rowan for the first and last time. He alone retains his costume as he releases her and she leads him into the waiting trap. It ends with Howie being consumed in the wicker man.

BEFORE MAY EVE

Historically less is known of Beltane than what is shown in the film. Even historians such as Ronald Hutton agree that the celebration itself has every mark of antiquity, although the details are sparse.[7] Beltane was characterized by fires to encourage the sun and crops along, but probably not to the extent that Frazer suggests in *The Golden Bough*. In order to make sense of *The Wicker Man*, we'll look at how it presents the day and try to sort fact from fiction.[8] *The Golden Bough* must be used with caution, as we'll see below.

To make sense of the passion of Sgt. Howie, we need to follow the Summerisle May Day in the order he experiences it. He arrives on Sunday, April 29.

Let's begin with Willow on the night of Howie's arrival. Sex will be the topic of our next chapter, but it's fair to say that May Day has long had a sexual element to it (Homans, 1970: 367). Howie hasn't yet been clued in to the importance of the date. Willow, like just about everyone on Summerisle, is named after a part of nature, namely a tree. This practice is intended to reflect the love of nature that Howie's Christianity sets out to domesticate (Ellis, 2002). Christians, as Howie notes when talking to the librarian, name their children from the Bible (although Neil, ironically, isn't a biblical name). Other than establishing scenes, followed by the offer of free love, the first day on the island is the preamble to the holiday. Keeping track of the days, for the original theatrical cut this would be Sunday; a "sabbath" filled with drinking, rowdiness, and sex is hardly what a Christian copper would expect or find acceptable.

MAY EVE

On May Eve (Monday, April 30), the next day, the first stop for Howie is the school, and here he has his first introduction to the maypole. Maypoles, according to present-day historians, did not have phallic associations in ancient times. This is a point of disagreement, of course, since in a Frazerian, or Freudian, analysis the connection is obvious. Nothing about the maypole, however, is simple. In Europe they could be used either on May Day or Midsummer. They could be cut fresh every year or they could be permanent structures in a town. The ribbons were a rather modern addition (Hutton, 1996: 233–35; Sermon in Franks et al., 2007). What do they represent? They're rather like Christmas trees in reverse. They represent nature with its potential to bloom. The most characteristic celebratory act was the dance around the maypole.

In *Wicker Man* the phallic association is made plain by the song the Schoolmaster leads as well as the explicit unison response of the girls inside. The maypole dance and song here represent preparation for the main celebration the next day. Even if historically the maypole was just a pole, the interpretation as a penis is accepted on Summerisle. Diegetically it works.

The woman nursing her baby in the graveyard while holding an egg—an act of sympathetic magic—is connected to the islanders' May Day perhaps by the suborning of the Easter egg symbol (itself quite likely borrowed from paganism). Recall that May Day supplants Easter as the spring seasonal festival. Howie's flashbacks the night before were to readings about what happened before the Crucifixion on what is called Maundy Thursday among Anglicans. That makes a connection to Easter. In fact, Easter was the previous Sunday in 1973. Historically no such egg rite is known specifically from May Day.

The interview with the gardener at the graveyard, although it reveals quite a lot about the pagan religion of Summerisle, doesn't focus directly on preparations for May Day. It does plant the idea that Rowan was murdered, but that could've taken place any day. The same may be said of putting a frog in one's mouth to cure a sore throat. It's sympathetic magic, not specific to May Day.

Finally, on his way to meet Lord Summerisle, Howie witnesses two fertility rites: pregnant women blessing blossoming fruit trees and naked girls dancing around and leaping over a bonfire. These are further instances of May Day preparation. Fires are a major element of historical Beltane celebrations. Although May Day has long been known as an occasion for trysts with lovers and the encouragement of fertility—such as the pregnant women touching the tree blossoms—there was historically no specific rite as the girls' "divinity lesson" as portrayed in *Wicker Man*. Diegetically, however, it serves both to shock Howie and to prepare the girls for the holiday. It again highlights the difference between Howie's religious understanding of incarnation versus that of the islanders—more on this in chapter 4, when we will also return to the interview with Lord Summerisle. The particular discussion isn't a focus on May Day but the background to it.

After exhuming "Rowan," Howie returns to Summerisle to declare he will be leaving in the morning to bring back more police. Summerisle informs him that it is for the best that he will be leaving, for May Day on the island will offend him. The day is thus bookended by references to May Day from Willow and Summerisle.

MAY DAY

The next day (Tuesday) is the holiday itself. Foiled from leaving by the sabotage of his plane, Howie is left to prevent Rowan's sacrifice by himself. As preparations are being made, he finds a book in the library that explains the pagan May Day rituals.[9] He will see them enacted. The three archetypal characters—the hobbyhorse, the male-female teaser, and the fool—do have associations with the holiday, or at least partially (Catterall and Wells, 2001: 125). We'll begin with the hobbyhorse.

Figure 6. Another trinity. © British Lion

Hobbyhorses, as children's toys, can't be traced historically any earlier than the fourteenth century. It is possible, of course, that children pretended to ride horses since the earliest days of their domestication (about 4000 BCE; Anthony and Brown, 1991). Their use in May Day celebrations probably goes back to medieval Britain, but not to pagan antiquity. The concept at play on Summerisle is to catch girls under the skirts of the horse to bless them with fertility. The hobbyhorse, however, also has the role of deciding the sacrifice in the chop game at the stone circle. This game is not, of course, a historical May Day custom.

The hobbyhorse, along with morris dancers and mummers, have had a history with May Day in the British Isles. All three were elements of celebration, each with their own backstory that space limitations prevent exploring fully.

The teaser has an association with a May Day hobbyhorse in Cornwall, where *Ritual* was set (Sermon in Franks et al., 2007). The male-female aspect, playing into the island's sexually charged holiday, is given ahistorical associations in *Wicker Man*. The Druid connection appears in the symbols Summerisle carries—sickle and mistletoe—which aren't necessarily part of the historically known teaser (Green, 2011: 27). The description seems to be based mostly on what Howie reads in the library book that morning. According to that description, Summerisle takes on that role as community leader.

Punch, "the most complex of all the symbolic figures," is indeed a complex blend in *Wicker Man*. Both his name and his costume identify him with Mr. Punch from the seventeenth-century British puppet show Punch and Judy (Collier, 2006: 9). His hooked nose and hunchback are distinctive, as is the slapstick he carries. Punch became a popular character in British culture in his own right, and he is here conflated with the fool. As an archetypal character the fool brings in very ancient associations. This is made explicit by adding his title "king for a day" in the film, which puts him in connection with ancient Mesopotamian customs of a day when the king was humiliated and a peasant reigned.[10] In a move worthy of *The Golden Bough*, such fools were killed after their day of (often mis-) rule.[11] Howie, unaware of this tradition, takes on Punch's role to try to rescue Rowan. Historically the character of the fool became associated with both morris dancers and sword dancers, thus bringing him into contact with actual May Day celebrations. We'll consider Punch more fully below.

The sword dancers, also outlined in the book Howie reads, reflect a very old art form that is attested pretty much worldwide. The specific knot made by interlacing the swords is a northern England custom (Sermon in Franks et al., 2007), but it isn't a form of sacrificial execution. In *Wicker Man* the dancers serve to build the tension as the May Queen, dressed as a hare, is beheaded. Although this is done to Holly (the May Queen) wearing a false head, Howie is convinced that it is one of the methods of "heathen barbarity" that the book had warned of.

Plot-wise, this does raise the question of how Howie intends to rescue Rowan (or in this case, Holly). His seaplane won't work and he would need to contact the mainland for any assistance. Since his radio is out of commission, he would likely need a phone box. His is indeed a fool's errand.

The May Queen is a figure with origins that reach far enough back to have become lost to historians. It's possible that the May Queen was originally the representation of an ancient goddess associated with spring and fertility, but since we lack clear beginnings of the tradition of crowning a May Queen, such ideas are speculative, even if popular. May Queens are mentioned from written records in the late Middle Ages (Homans, 1970: 354; Hutton, 1996: 238–39), too late to be intentional goddesses at that point. It's possible that earlier they were, but without written records indicating that, we can only wonder. In *Wicker Man* the May Queen is understated—she's but a small part of the ruse to trap Sgt. Howie.

Although fire plays a role, a wicker man was not generally part of a May Day or Beltane celebration, but remember the movie is about sacrifice. The final rituals involve an offering of a cask of ale to the unnamed sea god and an offering for the orchards, the climax of the film.

There are, of course, many religious details thrown into the cinematic version, some of which will be discussed in chapter 4, that give this May Day an aura of believability. In fact, much of May Day as presented in *Wicker Man* is either fiction or exaggeration meant to make a point. Celebrations of Beltane as in the old days had ceased long ago, and modern reconstructions of the holiday are based on events that aren't historically accurate. Religions are that way. A few of the elements stand out.

FIRE

It may appear so obvious that fire is a religious symbol that it goes without saying. It's worth pausing over it for a moment, however, because fire is frequently used as a source of horror—as in *Wicker Man* as well as in *Midsommar*—but part of that horror is based on its religious connotations.

Fire in horror has a long pedigree, including all three members of the folk horror trinity. In *The Blood on Satan's Claw* the demon is destroyed by fire at the end in a ritual context. It's not so much part of the horror as it is part of the pagan celebration that leads to the death of Angel (Linda Hayden) and of others prior to her. In *Witchfinder General* it's more explicit. One of the most horrific scenes is Matthew Hopkins' use of a ladder to lower a woman onto a blazing bonfire. Both of these are religious contexts.

The idea goes back at least as early as *Frankenstein*, when fire is used to destroy the monster, who is believed to be a sacrilegious abomination. In more modern horror it's still a common source of secular terror. Consider *Silent Hill* (Christophe Gans, 2006), *Mirrors* (Alexandre Aja, 2008), or even *The Lazarus Effect* (David Gelb, 2015). Fire has a distinctly religious element to it. Think of how in *Constantine* (Francis Lawrence, 2005) (and the Christian system from which it draws) the fires of Hell are literal. As in a form of the Prometheus myth, fire comes from the gods. *Wicker Man* makes religious fire entirely obvious by stating that Howie is to be a sacrifice.

Although whole burnt offerings—the kind that give us the word "holocaust"—existed in ancient times, the animals were dead before being burnt. Burning alive was reserved in the Middle Ages primarily for people who'd committed the most feared crimes, such as being witches (thus *Witchfinder General*). The fact that the horror of the fate was intense underlines the truly deplorable fact that it was used primarily against innocent people, often women (Roper, 2004). Although religions, including the Christianity behind the witch hunts, saw fire as purifying, it was nevertheless a source of terror.

The origins of purifying fire in Judaism, and subsequently in Christianity, perhaps came from Zoroastrianism, the oldest continually practiced religion known. A religion of ancient Iran that influenced both western and eastern religious traditions, it included a central tenet of fire as an element, if not *the* element, of purification. The fire that destroyed the wicked in that tradition was intended to purify as it did so. Although Christianity never developed a sacrificial system for animals, in Judaism the burning of the victims was considered rendering them to God. May Day on Summerisle shares that basic concept.

Ritual fires were part of all the known authentic ancient Celtic seasonal holidays— Beltane, Lughnasadh, Samhain, and Imbolc (Hutton, 1996). May Day, or Beltane, seems the most appropriate choice for the film because of how the death of the victim leads to the life of the crops, soon to follow in summer. The god of the sun, Nuada (more likely Belenus), is featured on Summerisle's flag. Belenus, historically, is one of the most worshipped of the old Celtic gods (Green, 2011: 142).

Gods have long been associated with fire. Agni, in Hinduism the deity whose name translates as "fire," is a major divinity. Even in Christianity the Holy Spirit is represented by fire. Prior to that, the use of a burning bush by Yahweh begins the process of building Judaism into a religion through Moses. Clearly fire had some divine associations in ancient Celtic beliefs as well. *Wicker Man*, however, uses fire sparingly until the actual wicker man appears.

Up to the point of ignition there are only small hints of threatening fire. The naked girls' leaping over a fire may be dangerous, but its purpose is benevolent. Nobody actually gets burnt. In the context of the movie it's important foreshadowing—the scene is shown several times from different angles. Apart from that ritual, the fire of the "hand of glory"—the candle made from a severed human hand—on May Day itself, as Howie naps, is small and non-threatening beyond the macabre question of its origin. Howie easily extinguishes it and even uses the candlestick, in good *Clue* fashion, as a weapon. Fire, however, is a signature feature of May Day. This misdirection in not showing it is key to the surprising, blazing end to the film.

Ari Aster's *Midsommar*, another example of both folk horror and holiday horror, takes place almost two months later in the year, at Midsummer, or Litha. The maypole and May Queen are prominent aspects of that story, as is fire. From a modern perspective each discrete holiday is branded with its own symbols, colors, and music. Ancient holidays generally shared liminal elements of celebration. Morris dancers and mummers were also part of holiday festivities in other real-life celebrations, not just Beltane or May Day. One thing that all of these elements have in common is that they represent stepping out of ordinary time into the sacred time of holidays. Perhaps this is best known regarding Samhain, or Halloween.

MASKING

Modern Halloween shares the feature of masking, as portrayed in *The Wicker Man*. Samhain was the start of a new year and a time when the barrier between this world and the spirit world was believed to be more permeable. The interaction of the dead with the living played a large role in Celtic "theology." It involves the unknown, a form of masking. We see nothing supernatural in *Wicker Man*, but clearly the islanders believe something significant is going on. They wouldn't sacrifice to gods they didn't believe in. This aspect of not knowing what rural folk believe plays into the folk horror color of the film, but also into holiday horror. It's also a form of masking. One of the reasons we anticipate holidays is that they are familiar to us. We know what to expect. Masking can frighten; children first encountering Santa Claus, for example, can be afraid of this costumed man.

Masking taps into some very deep roots in the shamanistic imagination (Heller-Nicholas, 2019: 27–37). This brief volume doesn't afford the space to analyze it in depth, but the trickster element is clearly part of it. Masking hides and reveals many truths about Summerisle.

Sergeant Howie is baffled by May Day from the moment he begins to experience it. Everything about the holiday suggests something unknown, unchristian. Disoriented, he's unable to realize that he is the beetle tied to the nail. Although the beetle is likely a form of sympathetic magic (Sermon in Franks et al., 2007), it too is going round and round the maypole nail. There's something threatening when you don't understand what other people's motivations are, unknowing as a beetle.

Scattered elements—fire, dancing, and disguising—seem to have been part of Celtic Beltane. The wearing of masks, like many of these elements, is known to modern people as part of Halloween. The tradition has complex roots (Morton, 2012), but the masks in *Wicker Man* again reflect the eeriness of not being able to see another person's facial expression. There's a more existential horror in masking, as it taps into religious motivations (Heller-Nicholas, 2019). Holiday horror often relies on masks. Would *My Bloody Valentine* be so scary if we could see Axel Palmer's face? Or would Leatherface be so frightening if he removed his mask? The islanders mask up on May Day. Arguably the most grotesque of the masks is that of Punch.

HOLY FOOLS

Punch is a "fool" and "king for a day." The character is well known in Britain from Punch and Judy shows, comedic puppet performances that feature the antics of Mr. Punch and his wife Judy. Although the puppets date back to the seventeenth century, *Wicker Man* plays more on the ancient aspect of Punch as a trickster (inherent in masking; Heller-Nicholas, 2019: 35–37). This idea reaches far back in history.

The "king for a day" motif, as I've indicated above, has an ancient pedigree. Societies as far back as those of ancient Mesopotamia seem to have had holidays that featured the king seeking a willing, and one suspects, naive temporary replacement. Taken up by later cultures, this transitory king was sometimes selected on the occasion of an eclipse. The person, generally a peasant, received royal treatment and honors. Until the danger passed. Being king for a day, however, came with a price. The folkloric end of the temporary monarch was sacrifice. Throughout history variations on this took place in literature and perhaps in some societies. Even if not historical (Hardy and Shaffer likely borrowed the idea from *The Golden Bough*), it contributes to the film's choice of Punch.

Obviously, in *The Wicker Man* diegesis, the fool isn't sacrificed annually. MacGregor notes that his costume gets tighter each passing year, and he's still very much alive. Indeed, the harvest has been fine since the time of Summerisle's grandfather. The holiday comes to its crisis point when something in the natural order has gone awry. Then May Day becomes a day of sacrifice. Liminal time can be dangerous. It's not a good time to be a fool.

Fools play a role in much of horror, and the holiday named after them, April Fool's Day, has its own movie (see chapter 1). Nobody knows for sure how April 1 came to be known as April Fool's Day (Wainwright, 2007: 3)—it's really hard to get the straight story since hoaxes on that very subject are often April Fool's pranks. The fact is, nobody knows. The suggestions of historians, however, point to religious origins.

Since the late Middle Ages people in the western world have treated April 1 as a day to send people on fool's errands or to play tricks on others (Chambers, 1864: 460–62; Bellenir, 2004: 271). Perhaps the most reasonable explanation is that the shifting of the Julian to the Gregorian calendar in the sixteenth century led to confusion among those who celebrated New Year's Day (traditionally March 25) incorrectly. The problem is that such an explanation has no direct connection with April 1. The calendar change was nevertheless religiously motivated, as Pope Gregory XIII was concerned about the effect the Julian calendar had on the date of Easter, since more precise measurements of the length of a day showed the error increasing over time.

Another contender for April Fool's is the Roman festival of Hilaria, celebrated over several days around March 25. Hilaria, as the name implies, was a festival of joy, likely welcoming spring. It was dedicated to the goddess Cybele (Magie, 1924: 250–51; Beard, North, and Price, 1998: 133–34). Again, this occasion didn't actually reach April

1, and there seems to have been no continuation of the holiday after Roman influence decreased. Unless, of course, April Fool's Day is a vestige of it. If it was, again, the origin is religious.

Although the movie *April Fool's Day* is entirely secular, it also plays on the fool theme. The entire movie is, of course, a set-up for the viewers as well as for most of the characters. As an example of holiday horror it doesn't really live up to anyone dying or the day being malevolent; still, it focuses firmly on the threatening nature of that day. It has a passing similarity to *Wicker Man* in that visitors are manipulated so that the scheme works.

The fool motif is time-honored in horror ("Don't open that door!" moments are ubiquitous). The intentional fool may, however, be complex. Consider Marty (Fran Kranz) from *The Cabin in the Woods*. Throughout the film, he's the loner on the holiday trip. He's openly a stoner, and although his friends don't make a big deal of it, he's comic relief. At the end, however, he saves Kristen (Dana Polk), while simultaneously dooming the world. The situation isn't dissimilar from *Wicker Man*. If Howie had been able to resist being sacrificed, crops would again fail. Marty manages to survive and the old gods are unleashed upon the world. The fool, as trickster, makes it difficult to pin down its May Day connection, beyond merriment.

The various elements of May Day are complex and many have origins lost to history. Did any of this really happen?

A BRIEF HISTORY CHECK

Wicker Man fandom is fond of noting that the film was well researched. At the same time, it's clear that much of the research can be traced back to James Frazer's wildly influential *The Golden Bough*. Single-volume abridgments are still commonly sold. Although scandalous when it came out, the influence of this multi-volume set is ubiquitous. In the magisterial third edition, published from 1906 to 1915, volumes 10 and 11 were dedicated to Balder, or rather, the fire rites of old Europe. This material was utilized by Hardy and Shaffer. The problem is that Frazer's method hasn't held up over time (Pettitt, 2005: 12; see also Krzywinska, 2000).

Anthropologists and historians today recognize that Frazer's theories were built on simple comparison. "This looks like that" isn't a sound way of tracing historical influence, let alone what actually happened. Also, his information gathering didn't utilize extensive fieldwork. Frazer's magnum opus, subtitled *A Study of Magic and Religion*, combined with the Jungian psychology reflected in the mythological works of Joseph Campbell, made popularly available a kind of monomyth of comparative cultures. Likewise, as popular as Campbell's work is, it hasn't fared well with critical studies. Part of the compelling nature of *The Golden Bough* is that we want it to be correct. It is deeply satisfying to see the patterns Frazer points out, despite their varied historical complications. Hardy and Shaffer's information about Beltane largely came from *The Golden Bough*. It was, and remains, extremely popular, even if historically inaccurate.

"In the central Highlands of Scotland bonfires, known as the Beltane fires, were formerly kindled with great ceremony on the first of May, and the traces of human sacrifice at them were particularly clear and unequivocal," Frazer wrote (1913, vol. 10: 146), without footnote. More historically grounded treatments are less sanguine about evidence for human sacrifice.[12] Human sacrifice did take place in antiquity, but it was a rare occurrence whose socially conditioned situations are poorly understood. Celtic culture seems to have used periodic human sacrifice (Green, 2011: 29–32). In other words, it may have happened occasionally, but we can't say exactly why.

Apart from Frazer's *Golden Bough*, it seems clear that some of the movie's information about Celtic religion comes from classical writers. Julius Caesar gave us the wicker man concept. The Roman historian Pliny the Elder, often considered unreliable, gave extended descriptions of Druidic traditions and included details such as harvesting mistletoe with a golden sickle—the two symbols Lord Summerisle, as the teaser, carries with him on the May Day procession (Hutton, 2009: 14). On Summerisle, May Day has a party atmosphere. Costumes, drinking, dancing, and free love make up the pagan practices that so trouble Howie's straitlaced Christianity. His religion has a lurking suspicion that underneath such celebratory events a deeper evil is lurking. He believes the sacrifice was (or will be) Rowan, but the only valid one was Jesus. His intolerant religion and that of Summerisle simply don't mix. Just like sex and holy days.

NOTES

1. The practice still continues. My first teaching post was at an Episcopalian seminary that, following Oxford University, divided the school year into Michaelmas Term and Easter Term instead of the usual fall and spring semesters.

2. Hutton (1996) is a major source for what follows on Celtic holidays; for Wiccan holidays see Bellenir (2004).

3. See Murray and Rolston (2008) on the title.

4. "The Final Cut" strangely has the maypole being crowned on May Eve and then again on May Day.

5. Since holidays are about time, we should note that the movie gives us no idea how the islanders mark weekends, if they do. Howie arrives on a Sunday, and Monday brings him into contact with teachers, a groundskeeper, and a librarian, all at work.

6. Many of these aspects are discussed in more detail in Richard Sermon's piece in Franks et al. (2007). See also Huckvale (2018: 155–56).

7. Hutton is widely recognized as the authority on ancient Britain. Marion Gibson also works in this area and directly addresses *The Wicker Man*. See Hutton (1991, 1996) and Gibson (2013).

8. Many of the details have been gathered by Richard Sermon—see his article in Franks et al. (2007).

9. The identity of the book is sometimes said to be Janet and Colin Bord's *Mysterious Britain*. As the Wicker Man wiki (https://twm.fandom.com/wiki/Props#Book_about_May_Day_in_the_library_Howie_reads.C2.A0) points out, the text read by Howie and the illustration do not occur in Bord. The glimpse of the text at the start of chapter 13 confirms that *Mysterious Britain* was used, but it isn't the source of the information as read.

10. Mesopotamian religion is notoriously complex, and there is controversy over how much, if any, of this took place historically. See Bidmead (2004: 79).

11. This is drawn from Frazer, and is historically disputed.

12. Frazer actually writes at length about the fires, the wicker man, and human sacrifice in his volumes on fire rites. Whether these actually took place or not has no material effect on the movie, which is fiction and a cautionary tale.

CHAPTER 3: SCARY SEX

Sergeant Howie's seaplane flies over the rocky, almost barren coast of the Hebrides. He passes the notorious Old Man of Storr on the Isle of Skye.[1] The landscape is forbidding and certainly not arable.

Figure 7. The Old Man—eyebrow, nose, chin at the upper left. © British Lion

After the credits' opening song comes Paul Giovanni singing "Corn Rigs." Taken from "The Rigs of Barley," a song by Scotland's national poet, Robert Burns, it celebrates trysts in the fields of harvest. The poem is actually based on the holiday of Lammas (Lughnasadh), which falls in August (see chapter 2). Nevertheless, the sexually evocative imagery fits what awaits the sergeant. Howie's first night on the island is suffused with sexuality. Islanders shamelessly (shamefully in Howie's eyes) make love in public. The bawdy "Landlord's Daughter" sung in the bar is clearly an attempt to offend the intended victim's staid views of sexuality. After Willow invites him to her room and he resists, the next morning he apologizes to her, saying he meant no offense, "Just that I don't believe in it, before marriage."

His first day searching for Rowan brings him to the school, where boys are dancing around a maypole as their teacher sings a song that would put an educator behind bars today. Even more shocking, Miss Rose's girls say "phallic symbol" in unison as Howie stands just outside the door. While all of this could be seen as mere titillation, such an interpretation overlooks the ancient connection between fertility and religion. Sex becomes a source of horror to the traditional, upright citizen fearing God's wrath. Without the attitudes Howie displays towards sex, the contrast could hardly have been as effective. This is reaffirmed by the frank sexuality of *Midsommar* and other folk horror, such as *The Blood on Satan's Claw*. On Summerisle sex is essential to May Day. Participation would save Howie but then his religion will condemn him eternally for it. Welcome to the scary sex of Summerisle.

RELIGION AND SEX

How can sex be scary? For all of us, up to a point in our lives it represents the unknown. Fear of the unknown is one of the most common and pragmatic of phobias. Once we gain that special knowledge, fear doesn't vanish. The very real fear of rape exists for women (as in *The Blood on Satan's Claw*) and men not uncommonly face "performance anxiety." Sex is a fraught activity.

Even so, that's not how *Wicker Man* makes it scary. Instead, it's an element intricately woven into the fabric of the holiday. It's the most obvious difference that sets the largely negative Christian view of life over against the free-love aesthetic of pagan Summerisle. Treatments of *The Wicker Man* sometimes breezily suggest that the sexual liberty of the islanders in simply part of the counterculture that arose in the sixties. While there is likely some truth in the counterculture aspect, this chapter makes the case that sexuality is integral to May Day as portrayed in the movie and that without it the contrast between Christianity and paganism falls apart.

The sexuality of *The Wicker Man* isn't gratuitous;[2] it's essential to May Day. In fact, the tension between Sgt. Howie's "traditional" Christianity and the open expression of "pagan" practice sets the action for the movie from the very beginning. To understand this the connection between sexuality and the cycles of nature must be explored.

Earth-centered religions, such as that constructed for Summerisle, celebrate the relationship between human sexuality and nature's fruitfulness. Typically this is called "sympathetic magic." Howie's refusal to participate marks him as the victim when those cycles break down.

Despite the Christian imagination that all of paganism is about sex, historically sex does tie closely with May Day because of its emphasis on fertility. While there are elements of sympathetic magic to this connection, they're part of a larger religious underpinning. Among cultures worldwide—and this isn't a Frazerian oversimplification—there is a belief in cause and effect. This extends to the idea that human actions, through the manipulation of specific aspects of nature, influence what happens in the world without any direct physical connection. Although scholars raised in a culture heavily influenced by an often-forgotten Christianity (this applies to all of western Europe and many of its former colonies) see this as superstition—Einstein's "spooky action at a distance"—for indigenous peoples it is more a matter of believing in a close connection between the earth and those who live on it. Remember, many of these belief systems are earth-centered (Magliocco, 2003).

How exactly do "earth-centered" religions explain this? Religions such as the major monotheistic traditions (Judaism, Christianity, Islam) believe in revelation. That is, religious information comes down from God, and since there is only one God that information is, by definition, correct. On the other end of the spectrum, earth-centered religions, while often recognizing gods, see humans as an integral part of nature. Rather than specially created by a single god, religious truth is found in learning our place in being part of the earth. There is wisdom in the environment and it isn't constrained to the dictates of science (which are based on a Christian worldview). Sex is written into nature and therefore appropriate, even necessary, for religion (Urban, 2006).

What scholars call "sympathetic magic" is a religious belief that a human action can influence something in nature. It is understood that we are all organically connected by virtue of being part of the earth. Like affects like. Therefore, human sexuality inspires fertility in the crops. You've no doubt noticed by now that *Wicker Man*'s religion is a blend of ideas. Young girls jump over a fire to become pregnant. Women who became pregnant the old-fashioned way bless the apple blossoms. These ideas are mutually exclusive only if there is one god who declared it happens only one way. Parthenogenesis isn't a contradiction to human sexuality inspiring nature. They are both perspectives on regeneration. Remember, the main conflict in *Wicker Man* is between incompatible religions.

Keep in mind that the May Day celebration on Summerisle isn't an accurate portrayal of any single historic practice. It does give us privileged insight, however, into what the fictional islanders believe. Their belief in sacred time is widely shared among actual indigenous religions as well as by Christianity. "There is a time for every purpose," wrote the author of Ecclesiastes (3.1) in the Bible, and on Summerisle, May Day is the time for sex.[3] Of all the holidays of the reconstructed pagan year, May Day is the most suited to encouraging fruitfulness since it's associated with planting after winter.

Midsommar also brings sexuality into the picture for a June holiday, but there's a logic to that as well. *Midsommar* is set in the far north of Sweden—far enough north for the nights to remain light. (That factor is one of the elements driving the horror. It distorts the perceptions of reality where sleep is constantly interrupted.) Another factor here is that growing seasons are much shorter in such northern latitudes. Fertility concerns in a region with a much later planting season would fall later in the year. Besides, the religious commune, the Harga, doesn't follow the Celtic calendar presented in *Wicker Man*. Both movies' fertility concerns involve sex. When Christian (Jack Reynor) does sleep with Maja (Isabelle Grill), it leads to his death, the opposite of what happens with Sgt. Howie. Both are examples, two of many, of scary sex.

SCARY SEX

Scary sex isn't unique to *Wicker Man*. Indeed, sexual anxiety is often used in horror (Cowan, 2021). It occurs in the trinity of early folk horror—somewhat mutedly in *Witchfinder General*, but pretty obviously in *The Blood on Satan's Claw*. The rape scene of Cathy Vespers (Wendy Padbury) is truly scary from several angles. *Re-Animator* (Stuart Gordon, 1985), *Antichrist* (Lars von Trier, 2009), *Lovely Molly* (Eduardo Sánchez, 2012), even *Species* (Roger Donaldson, 1995) (and even more so *Species II* [Peter Medak, 1998]), for example, have scenes where sex itself can be terrifying. *Re-Animator* is infamous for its decapitated oral sex scene. He (Willem Dafoe) and She (Charlotte Gainsbourg) in *Antichrist* are making passionate love when their toddler son slips and falls from a window, setting up the horror for the rest of the film. The sexual mutilation scene that takes place at the cabin is particularly intense. *Lovely Molly* features a scene where Molly (Gretchen Lodge) seduces her minister only to get him naked and gruesomely murder him in the act. *Species II* may be better classified as science fiction, but the scene where Patrick Ross (Justin Lazard) impregnates two women only to have the "species" burst from them immediately afterward illustrates the point as well.

Clearly sex is used in some films for titillation. Beyond the salacious aspects, sex is sometimes legitimately part of the horror. *It Follows* (David Robert Mitchell, 2014) is an especially good example of this. It's integral to the story. While not holiday horror, *It Follows* could arguably be folk horror set in a suburban landscape of a suffering Detroit. The undefined "it" follows young people who've had sex with a person it's already following. The only way to get it off your trail, temporarily, is to pass it along to someone else. The sex isn't incidental—it's integral to the story.

The same is true of *The Wicker Man*, only in the context of holiday horror. The sex has to be kept in tension with Sgt. Howie remaining a virgin, however. This creates a voyeuristic element to his character. Christianity early on introduced "sin" as an element of sexuality. Judaism, out of which Christianity grew, promoted modesty regarding sex, but appropriate sex was hardly considered sinful. The Roman Empire, into which Christianity emerged, was fairly open about sexuality; many of its holidays featured sexual elements. Christianity established itself as a counterculture with its emphasis on avoiding sex. If sex had to be part of life, it should at least not be enjoyable. This idea took hold to the point that both Catholic and Protestant forms of Christianity shared a deep ambivalence about sex. Not all Christian sects feared sex in the same way (Endsjø, 2011).

Sergeant Howie is portrayed as an Anglican. His attitudes, however, are more in line with Puritanism. While Puritans weren't opposed to sexuality within marriage, anything that suggested or promoted it outside of those bounds was vehemently rejected. Although Puritans as such were no longer a separate denomination during the Victorian era, when photography first began to develop, the cultures—both British and American—that grew out of Puritan sensibilities objected strongly to pornography (Giesberg, 2017; Marcus, 2017). Not only did the portrayal of nudity violate their scriptural sensitivities (which was bad enough),[4] it also encouraged extra-marital sexual exploration. Any public display of sexually suggestive material, in combination with Victorian sensibilities, became not only distasteful but sinful.

The sexual revolution of the 1960s slowly changed attitudes toward sex in cultures influenced by Puritan ideals, but deep-seated fears still attended sex itself. Some psychological, but some clearly theological (Endsjø, 2011). Generations of teaching regarding divine displeasure at sex was, and remains, part of the upbringing of many Christians. While those attitudes have eroded over time, they were still prevalent in the 1970s. The growing cult following of *The Wicker Man* suggests that they may well remain intact today—or are at least recognized. On some level many Christians still believe sex to be at best profane, if not sinful (DeRogatis, 2014).

While the May Day—and religion—of Summerisle was fabricated for the movie, the integration of sexuality into holidays is in keeping with pre-Christian attitudes. Without the "one true God" giving strict instructions about and advice against sex, some other religions saw it as a cause for celebration. To Howie's Christian point of view, this is a deviant outlook on sexuality. Deviance, before more recent emphases on diversity and inclusion, was considered problematic in its own right. Sexuality was to be policed for fear of offending God. Otherwise it's difficult to explain why so many sex acts between consenting adults remained illegal into modern times. Or why so many books have been written on sex and fear, many of them trying to bring Christians toward a more contemporary view of what's healthy. The pagans of Summerisle, retaining their old religion, have overcome this fear. There is no fiery Hell awaiting them in the afterlife should they indulge in deity-angering sex. For the fear to work in the movie, the audience should mostly have not made that theological move. Hell must remain a possibility. Without it Howie could easily have saved himself by accepting Willow's invitation.

By its very nature, human sex involves vulnerability. Although the danger element—apart from sexually transmitted diseases—is largely underplayed in contemporary cinema, that was not the case in 1973. Yes, films had been made exploiting nudity and presenting sexually explicit scenes. *Deep Throat* released in 1972, for example, to predictable furor. For mainstream cinema, however, there was still quite a lot of caution around sex in that time frame (Krzywinska, 2006). *The Wicker Man*, along with *The Blood on Satan's Claw*, made it part of the horror. In the latter, for example, Angel's stripping off her clothes before Reverend Fallowfield (whose name is significant)[5] is met by him with both temptation and horror. He fears violating the Christian principles that define his life. His very soul is in peril!

It may be difficult to conceptualize this in the present, but when the threat to a person's soul was real and serious, no greater terror could've been invoked. Eternal punishment was, well, eternal. The simultaneous desire and doom make sex a fraught element in such films. *Wicker Man* loses a good deal of its draw if Howie is merely blasé about the dangers of sexuality. This is one of the key differences between the movie and David Pinner's *Ritual*—in the novel, Hanlin seriously considers sex with Anna to the point of going into her room and calling her name on the night of her attempted seduction (chapter 9). Hanlin isn't appalled by the very thought. Howie, although tempted, is. Sex outside of marriage isn't venial. The fact that he's engaged makes it adultery, and as such is potentially liable to punishment by death (Leviticus 20.10) or worse, to a Bible-believer such as himself. This is scary sex indeed.

SEX: DEVIANT OR SACRED?

"Deviant" sexuality frequently serves the purpose of horror auteurs (Halberstam, 1995; Ingebretsen, 2001; Clover, 2015; Cowan, 2021). Given modern mores and standards, there's nothing really deviant about adult consensual sex. In some jurisdictions certain sex acts may be technically illegal, but largely because of the success of the counterculture at the time of *Wicker Man*, they're not really seen so much as deviant as individualized (Endsjø, 2011). Nevertheless, the incipient Christian culture still sees holidays as sacred time. Every year, for example, "keep Christ in Christmas" campaigns crop up in the United States. Even secular holidays take on an aura of the sacred. Adding sex to a sacred occasion makes it seem deviant in this context. While Valentine's Day might be pointed out as a counterexample, it's more the exception that proves the rule.

Valentine's Day was originally a saint's day (dedicated to an uncertain St. Valentine) and may have originally been promoted to counter the Roman festival of Lupercalia (Forbes, 2015: 46–47). Roman holidays, as opposed to Christian outlooks on sacred occasions, encouraged sex. Think of what adult Valentine cards hint, or state outright. Roman religion, like the pre-Christian "Celtic" religion of Summerisle, freely incorporated sex into its practice. This applied especially to holidays, when the constraints of normal daily life were relaxed. Christianity didn't share that celebration of sex.

Christian holidays often became solemn, church-attending occasions. The purpose was to get a celebrator's mind off of the things of this world such as food, money, and sex. Focusing on the spiritual aspects of the saints, including Valentine (whichever Valentine he was), served to prevent "sin." And remember, by the time of Augustine in the fifth century, sex itself had become sinful. Indeed, it was the original sin. (It isn't that way in the Bible, but Augustine won out over the Good Book on this particular point.) Sex on a holy day ("holiday") was pretty deviant.

In the Hebrew Bible (also known as the "Old Testament") there are prohibitions about sex before or during holy occasions. Although Judaism never developed the antipathy to sex that characterized Christianity, clearly sex was considered immodest, or at least overly indulgent at certain times. In other words, it was inappropriate for certain sacred times. Other pre-Christian religions obviously disagreed. Sex itself was to be celebrated, and, in a sense difficult to wrap modern minds around, it was sacred (Goldberg, 1930: 4–5).

Although we've been considering holy days and sacred occasions, we haven't really considered what exactly "holy" and "sacred" denote. At its basic root, "holy" indicates a quality of "otherworldliness" (Otto, 1922). "Sacred" refers to something set apart for use with the holy. In other words, sacred things were dedicated to encounters with the holy, which weren't everyday occurrences. (If every day was a holiday, what would make such holy days special?) In the worldviews that developed out of the Bible, the holy and the sacred came to be associated with the "one true God." Using sacred things for unholy purposes profaned them, and in the biblical world this could be deadly.

That doesn't mean that the ideas of holiness or sacredness developed only in the Good Book. People around the world recognized sacred objects, sacred places, and sacred times. No civilization exists on record that does, or did, not recognize some kind of sacred time, even if couched in secular terms. How such times are celebrated, however, varies widely depending on the culture. The use of sex in sacred ceremonies isn't universal, but it certainly isn't uncommon. It was the ethical systems that developed out of the monotheistic religions (Judaism, Christianity, and Islam) that largely created the idea of sex as a problem.[6] Sinful peccadilloes were more than just bad social conventions in monotheistic eyes; inappropriate sex especially angered God. Indeed, many other sins could be venial, but deviant sex, along with murder, is among the top two. To put sex in a holiday was well-nigh unthinkable. And yet Sgt. Howie finds himself in precisely that scenario. Surrounded by pagans who prepare for and celebrate their holidays with sex, his world has been turned upside down.

HOLIDAY SEX

Holidays, from a Christian perspective, are sexless celebrations to remind believers of chaste saints and events in the "history of salvation." What is the "history of salvation"? Again, this requires a specifically Christian outlook.

The idea developed early on in Christianity that Jesus was part of a predetermined plan that God had worked out from the very beginning of time itself. Taking events of the Bible as their cue, theologians began to reconstruct what they thought that plan was. Since Jesus was central to it, and since Jesus was here to save humanity, this mapping of events led to the concept of the history of salvation. Important points of that "history" came to be celebrated, giving us holy days.[7] Eventually, as the church started to celebrate more and more post-biblical events and people, nearly every day of the year became the commemoration of some saint or other. So much so that some days have more than one saint to recognize.

Not all such holidays were celebrated with equal vigor, however. Major holidays— masses—stood out from the mundane saints' days. And often the dates of major events in "salvation history" were moved to coincide with pre-Christian holidays. May Day became the commemoration of St. Walpurga, in Christian calendars.[8] Other examples are better known: Christmas was fixed in December largely because of the various Roman festivals, such as Saturnalia, that took place then. All Saints, also known as All Hallows, was moved to November 1 to compete with Samhain, and thus gave us autumnal Halloween. Obviously the history of salvation doesn't follow a strictly historical calendar.

Particularly sacred or holy days, or even seasons—such as Lent—came to be associated with self-denial rather than self-indulgence. Even Thanksgiving was originally a day to spend in church rather than a day to overeat. Indeed, the enjoyable things of life, if pursued too much, became "deadly sins." Consider gluttony, sloth, or lust. Too much eating, sleeping, or lovemaking will lead to damnation. No wonder Sgt. Howie simply can't comprehend a holiday that encourages sex. It turns the Christian idea of holy days on its head.

Over time, various minor attempts have been made to Christianize Beltane, or May Day. It became a day for special remembrances of Mary, "the blessed virgin," "full of grace" (from the Catholic rosary). It also became associated with Jesus' other chaste parent as the feast of St. Joseph the Worker. It may come as no surprise, then, that May Day is the Labor Day of parts of eastern Europe.[9] Probably the most widespread European connection became that of St. Walpurga, Walpurgisnacht being the best-known celebration (Bellenir, 2004: 271). Never was there a major effort to supplant Beltane.

There is no patron saint of sex. The fact that a religion has a holiday celebrated with sex is completely disorienting to someone of Puritan outlook like Sgt. Howie. Dismissive of other views ("Ach, what is all this? I mean, you've got fake biology, fake religion… Sir, have these children never heard of Jesus?"), he can't see that sexuality is possibly a fact of life to celebrate in its own right. Making Howie Anglican puts him firmly between Protestant and Catholic. And firmly outside the comfort zone of sex for religious purposes.

Pagan celebrations were often held up as examples of debauches that would offend either a Catholic or a Puritan deity. This isn't a new idea. Even the Bible portrays those who worship different gods as overly lustful. Some ancient religions did indeed celebrate sex. In ancient Mesopotamia, for example, there was a symbolic ritual of "sacred marriage" where a king copulated with a priestess (Nissinen and Uro, 2008). The striking difference here is that of attitude—sex in the context of religious celebration is discounted in the Bible. We've seen how that translated into a sterile Christianity.

FERTILITY

May Day has, at least since the medieval period in the British Isles, been associated with fertility (Homans, 1970: 367; Hutton, 1996: 228). This association is not likely to have evolved within Christianity. When two religions meet, after the believers are done trying to kill each other, they start to blend. This has happened time and time again. Often, especially in monotheism, there comes a point at which one group will claim to have the "pure" religion (there is no "pure" religion that hasn't been influenced by other religions) and will declare all others heretical. This splintering even continues on down the path of denominations within the same religion, let alone a completely foreign belief system.

May Day has all the signs of a fertility holiday having developed prior to Christianity but then having started to blend with it. Celtic religion has a strong interest in fertility (Green, 2011: 69). *Wicker Man* tries to present a May Day reconstructed after Christianization. Remember, Summerisle says that the ministers fled when his grandfather's experiments proved successful. The islanders were Christians who are now trying to recapture their pagan heritage. There are subtle cinematic references to this Christianity in the film. One is where Howie is being led, clad in a white shift, to the wicker man. At one point he stumbles, framed very much like the station of the cross where Jesus falls twice on his way to execution.

Figure 8. Howie stumbles. © *British Lion*

This blending becomes obvious in a couple other scenes as well. One is where Howie interviews the graveyard keeper (Aubrey Morris). He asks about the islanders' minister, and as the keeper incredulously laughs "Minister?" the cross atop the ruined church in the background is framed behind his head, slightly out of focus. This is a formerly Christian culture that still uses church grounds. As Howie interviews the librarian about the death certificate of Rowan Morrison, he notes May's parents had names from the Bible. "Yes, they were very old," the librarian counters. Christianity is ancient history on Summerisle.

Even the May Day researched by Howie in the library is a blending of cultures as well as sexualities. The figure specifically of Punch dates only to the Middle Ages—the fool is, of course, much older than that—but Punch's context was a Christianized England. The exaggerated codpiece of the Punch costume (clearly seen when MacGregor dons it) emphasizes the importance of sex to the day.[10] Punch uses his bladder to slap the three women's behinds after they approach him with clappers that intimate sexual play. The hobbyhorse, worn by Oak (Ian Campbell), is associated not only with the large penises of horses but also the capturing of girls under his skirt, seen only briefly in the movie, as a fertility ritual, not connected with Punch. The ambiguous sexuality of the teaser both underscores the importance of sex to May Day and the breakdown of neat Christian categories. All of these elements are part of the blended holy history of the sexual May Day of Summerisle.

RELIGION AND SEX

The technique of a religion condemning other religions based on their sexual mores is familiar from the Bible, as noted. The cultural tendency to see one's own culture as normal and others as debased, although problematic, is natural enough. Evolution has acted differently on groups long separated by geographical features, so that the ethics of one's own group seem "natural" while those of foreigners seem "strange." Often "immoral." Or "perverted." This is just how Howie interprets it, although this separation is only by a century or so.

The Bible, particularly the Hebrew Bible, is surprisingly open to sex within one's own community. Yes, there are incest prohibitions and laws against rape and adultery, but the overall effect is one of sex as not a bad thing. It's important to keep in mind that in biblical times overpopulation wasn't a problem. Many, many children didn't survive beyond five, and women often died in childbirth, frequently in their twenties. In order to keep a population going, quite a bit of sex was required. Judaism, while regulating some sexual relationships, never developed the antipathy toward procreation that Christianity later instilled in its religious practice and thinking. It wouldn't have made sense to do so.

Although the New Testament reflects a somewhat later world, the situation hadn't much changed regarding human populations. Death in childbirth remained common, as did infant mortality. The shift toward negative sex seems to have accompanied a view reaching out into the non-Jewish world. Paul of Tarsus, who is largely responsible for Christian attitudes towards sex, was a missionary to Asia Minor and southern Europe. Many of his converts weren't Jewish. This raises the concern of differing sexual mores. All of these different cultures were under Roman occupation, and Roman society had largely positive ideas regarding sex. For Paul the problem was primarily theological.

Paul was convinced that Jesus (who had died before Paul became a believer) would be returning any day now—two millennia ago. He didn't go as far as condemning sex itself, but he advised holding out a bit longer because the wait would be brief. Sex would be a distraction. Christianity grew to be otherworldly in its early days. Not having much success in gaining political clout, it was illegal in the Roman Empire and you could die if you were caught practicing it (Moss, 2014). In such circumstances it makes good sense to be otherworldly. Not only that, but early Christians expected the end of the world at any moment. That also feeds into the idea of denial. Why indulge in sex when that means you must marry—a long-term commitment—and Jesus could return any moment now? Better to deny the urge to be caught in the middle of something that was quickly becoming sinful in its own right. If you do give in, it's shameful and must be kept as hidden as possible. This view obviously didn't apply to those who believed differently.

Those isolated from neighboring cultures—illustrated in *Wicker Man* by making them islanders—handle sexuality differently. The only thing that makes sexual practices deviant is comparison with one's own traditions. Christianity's staid outlook on the subject meant that just about any variation would be considered highly offensive. By the 1970s Christianity had nearly two millennia of teaching about the evils of sex. Sex may be directly utilized in religion, as in the case of some aspects of tantra in Hinduism and Buddhism, for example (Endsjø, 2011). Comparatively, Christian reticence towards sex is really the odder outlook. It is a religion that encourages general denial in a way most religions leave for advanced practitioners.

Nothing marks the citizens of Summerisle as "pagans" so much as their lack of shame regarding sexuality—this reflects counterculture outlooks, but also religious perspectives. The complete lack of shame has a stunning effect on Sgt. Howie. May Day, with its exultation of sex and reproduction, seems extremely atavistic to his "developed" and unquestioned Christian outlook. Not only that, it seems entirely too casual to his eyes.

One of the striking scenes of *It Follows*—perhaps the most self-aware of recent sex and horror films—is where Jamie (Jay, played by Maika Monroe) is explaining to Paul (Keir Gilchrist) that she'd slept with Greg (Daniel Zovatto) before, in high school. "It was no big deal," she says laconically. To think the May Day sex on Summerisle is casual, however, is to miss the point. There's a sense that since sex is pleasurable and fun it must be somehow shallow. That outlook tends to be behind casual sex. It's very far from what happens among the islanders. Howie's misreading of its significance is fatal.

May Day on Summerisle explores many angles of this. Couples making love in public (with the women on the top), girls dancing naked hoping for parthenogenesis, Willow serving as the community's sexual gateway, the maypole representing the male role in becoming once again a tree, pregnant women blessing apple blossoms, even shrubbery trimmed to phallic shapes—all of this suggests a considerable depth of understanding, an almost Kinseyian level of theology. Sex is deeply integrated into the islanders' religion. Let's consider each of these briefly.

Couples, well, copulating in public is shameful to Howie. Although it's not biblical, the biblically inspired legend of Lilith underscores the problem. In one version of the legend, Lilith, Adam's first wife, was banished from Eden for wanting to be on top during sex. Since the driving role was considered a male prerogative, this kind of radical equality was considered sinful and inappropriate, according to the legend (Schwartz, 1988). Even if Howie knows nothing of Lilith, the fact that sex is being performed openly and without shame taxes his understanding. From a pagan perspective, the sexes are equal partners with, as the next instance shows, males perhaps being unnecessary.

Parthenogenesis, Howie's "fake biology," is, as Lord Summerisle explains, an ancient and venerable tradition. Not only does it occur in the New Testament with Mary, but ancient pre-biblical religions knew of several virgin goddesses who were also mothers. This physical impossibility (at least at that time) was a mystery worthy of the gods. Human experience tells us pregnancy doesn't work that way, and yet it remains a religious hope on Summerisle. Howie doesn't receive Summerisle's comparison with Christianity well. In fact, he doesn't even try to answer it. The virgin birth isn't called parthenogenesis among the Christian faithful. It's considered a singular miracle that changed salvation history. On Summerisle it remains an open possibility on May Day.

Willow has the role of teaching young men the joys of sex. In Pinner's novel Anna Spark, who is killed by Hanlin, is a genuine nymphomaniac. Willow has a more quasi-official position among the islanders, as is made explicit by the harbour master's song. She ensures that by May Day there are no eligible adult males who've not contributed to the fertility ritual. Human effort reminds nature to be fertile. Nobody on Summerisle is referred to as being married. Refusal to participate indicates that someone holds their own plans above those of the community. What's being asked is, after all, pleasurable rather than onerous.

Not only is the maypole explained explicitly as a phallic symbol in the movie, but the Schoolmaster's song emphasizes the cycle of nature. The tree houses a bird that provides the feather for a bed. The bed brings the girl and man together, leading to a boy who becomes a man whose grave houses a tree. Sex has an obvious place in this endless cycle, and to remove it is to break the circle. Sex is fully integrated in May Day, and to remove it is to do violence to the holiday.

Sympathetic magic is evident again as the pregnant women bless the apple blossoms. Like begets like and fruit leads to fruit. True, the sex that led to pregnancy was in the past, but the desired end result is the fruitfulness of the enterprise. The women who've carried babies to this late term have influence on the trees to do the same. The phallic topiary plays a similar role, but from the masculine side of the equation. Summerisle uses sex to its fullest religious significance. Howie sees it all as vulgar. And frightening. Although engaged he won't have sex until the church sanctions it, after marriage.

Finding oneself in a society with completely different values triggers fears of the unknown. Howie, as a virgin, would likely know the anxiety of the uninitiated. The less wary, far from home where a fiancée is unlikely ever to know—being the wrong kind of sacrifice—would give in to temptation. Fear of sex in some ways equates to fear of God. After all, according to historians, May Day was traditionally a time to take a partner out into the fields, far from prying eyes (Hutton, 1996: 228). On Summerisle being a sexually mature virgin is deviant.

FULL PARTICIPATION

The worlds of Christianity and paganism clash over their understanding of what pleases the gods on holy occasions. Sergeant Howie, by not participating in the promotion of Summerisle's fertility the traditional pleasurable way, must participate by being a sacrifice. As shown in the flashbacks, Howie's religion—recall that his Bible reading focuses on the springtime holiday of Maundy Thursday, the prelude to Easter—sets up the differences between solemn holidays spent in church and the exuberant nature holidays spent outdoors.[11] This sets the two holidays in direct opposition—but that doesn't mean they share nothing in common.

Easter is the celebration of resurrection with nary a naughty thought in mind, while May Day is also a celebration of the resurrection of nature but with people showing the way it's done. The sober, if joyful, nature of Easter is, perhaps unwittingly, also interlaced with fertility. The Easter Bunny, as a character, reflects the abundance of rabbits at the onset of spring. Rabbit gestation periods are only a month long. This natural fertility is a springtime symbol. Or consider the Easter egg. Were it not for the dressing up of these eggs as resurrection symbols, their sexual nature would be completely obvious. Easter is a theologically enhanced fertility celebration (Forbes, 2015: 95–100).

Sergeant Howie's Bible reading, however, contrasts with Willow's naked dance next door. This is one of the virtues of the theatrical release—the contrast between reading the Bible and receiving communion utilizes polar opposites: piety or a night of fornication. The Christian sublimation of springtime's natural signals at Easter mirrors the sublimation of Howie's sexuality—if ignored it can be dangerous. He's an uptight officer, a gallant fellow.

May Day on Summerisle requires full adult participation: either you "cut some capers" or you get brought to the gods' attention as a sacrifice. Everyone on the island is involved. Even the children (in a weak reflection of Pinner's *Ritual*) wear masks and mislead Howie on his frantic search for Rowan. Those capable and of age have sex.

This is perhaps best illustrated with the chop sequence. Six sword dancers arrange their blades into an interlaced star—a symbol of the sun. When the islanders reach the stone circle, each must put their head in the center of the star while everyone else chants

"Chop! Chop!" Howie, concerned that Rowan will be sacrificed this way, is suddenly seized by the nose—he's wearing the Punch costume. "Everyone must go through, MacGregor," Lord Summerisle admonishes. "It's a game of chance." The important point is that all must participate.

Figure 9. Willow's religion. © British Lion

Failing to take part in a major festival can lead to exclusion from the community. In the Bible the most obvious example involves the Feast of Unleavened Bread, which was eventually merged with Passover. Anyone who eats leavened bread during this festival will be cut off from their people (Exodus 12.19). This is an example of a full participation requirement. In some forms of Christianity there are "days of obligation" during which you must attend mass—these without fail occur on holidays. In other words, religions are quite familiar with the concept of required holiday participation. By joining in you're confirming that you are part of the group (Johnston, 2015: 140).

Other holiday horror also uses this trope as well. *April Fool's Day*, for example, requires that each of the friends visiting Muffy St. John gets "killed" over the weekend. *Halloween* has all the friends, with the exception of the final girl Laurie Strode, being murdered. The same applies to *Midsommar*. Participation is required.[12]

The nature of holidays suggests as much. It's the day that is holy. Whether someone joins in or not isn't a matter of preference, but of pleasing the gods. Those who don't do what the gods want have a long history of being thrown into the fire. If, when he was researching May Day, Sgt. Howie had studied the nature of holidays in general he would likely have saved his life. *Wicker Man* makes excellent use of the fear associated with entering a culture where everyone else shares a religion unlike one's own. Religions, after all, are community-building tools. What Howie can't see is that sex can also be used to build a community. Indeed, that sex can be a religious requirement.

What Howie overlooks is that a society decides what is acceptable. Christianity has long conditioned people to believe that a religion is revealed from above, whereas religions are now understood to be human responses to their environment. Morality is what a society determines it is.[13] Howie can't accept a culture where Christian mores don't rule supreme. Where chaste Christian views of holidays don't prevail. A religion with a holiday where sex is central. That inability to think outside the box is his death sentence. When your own religion forbids it, sex can be very scary. Deadly, even.

COMPARE *MIDSOMMAR*

The choice of May Day over David Pinner's choice of Midsummer sharpens the focus on sexuality. Midsummer doesn't have the sexual focus that Beltane does. Midsummer is about lack of darkness, of the almost oppressive nature of too much light. This is evident in Ari Aster's *Midsommar*. It's both folk horror and holiday horror, like *Wicker Man*. Both films focus on outsiders trying to understand a completely different culture—one that has a more open sexuality as well as having a propensity for burning things.

Midsommar also presents scary sex, but in a different way. As the five friends travel to the Harga in Sweden, Mark (Will Poulter) is overly vocal about seeking sex. In fact, he tries to pressure Christian into leaving Dani (Florence Pugh), suggesting he might want to find a girlfriend who actually likes sex. It's no wonder that their fates are sealed by their penises. Urinating on a sacred tree leads Mark to his death. It's more complicated for Christian. He's thinking of leaving Dani and she's worried that she's losing him. Among the Harga, inbreeding is a problem and outsiders are needed to refresh the gene pool. Christian is selected.

Maja, one of the Harga girls, has been subtly hitting on him since he arrived. While Dani is off seeing to her May Queen duties (more on this in a moment), Christian is led to a hut where he has ritual sex with Maja, all the while under the influence of the drugs the Harga liberally spice the visitors with. Adding to the confusion of the outsiders is the lack of darkness. Sleep deprivation and inability to tell at a glance whether it's day or night creates a heady mix of irrationality. Dani is shown Christian's infidelity, and his fear upon running naked from the hut is evident. His sexual episode leads directly to his death. Dani, as May Queen, has to select a victim for ritual burning.

Why is Dani May Queen at Midsummer? Remember, pre-Christian holidays weren't always branded as starkly as modern ones are. We know from the merest glance whether it's Christmas, Easter, or Halloween.[14] In the days before commercialization of holidays, many of them were celebrated in similar ways—feasting (or fasting), dancing (or praying), communal gathering. Some elements appear in different holidays, such as the maypole and the May Queen. Both are part of May Day, but in some cultures also part of Midsummer. Seasons are, after all, timed variably at different latitudes. *Midsommar* presents a holiday similar to May Day, but in a different context, with more obvious violence.

In the British context, Midsummer lacked the fertility associations so strongly present at May Day. Nor has Midsummer been celebrated with the same vigor as May Day. While either technically could've been used, May Day has the associations of blooms, blossoms, and scary sex. The sympathetic magic associated with May Day pervades the idea of human sexuality encouraging the fertility of crops. By Midsummer fruits are already ripening and don't really require much encouragement.[15]

To pull all of this together requires consideration of another species of horror: theology. What kind of religious thinking makes May Day a time for killing strangers in a horrific way?

NOTES

1. There is a visual joke here that tour books seldom mention. "The Old Man of Storr" is a rocky pinnacle that juts from the landslip in an obvious way. From not too great a distance, however, the Storr itself resolves into an uncanny profile of an old man's face. The man is lying on his back, making the typical "Old Man" his erect penis. This profile of the old man's face can be seen, in a brief glimpse, in the aerial sequence over Skye in the film opening.
2. Much has been written on horror and sex. To start see Halberstam (1995), Clover (2015), and Cowan (2021).

3.   While the "text" for this book is the theatrical release, the director's cut and the final cut underscore this point by having Lord Summerisle bringing Ash Buchanan (Richard Wren) to be initiated by Willow on Howie's first night on the island. Summerisle contrasts the ways of nature—the snails—with Christianity.

4.   Jesus famously stated that even looking at a woman lustfully was the same as adultery (Matthew 5.28).

5.   A field that is fallow is one that hasn't been plowed for planting. Its virginal significance is almost as clear as is that of Sgt. Howie. See Evans-Powell, 2021: 87–88.

6.   Some other religions caution against reproduction for theological reasons, but don't have an antipathy to sex itself.

7.   Holy days obviously predated Christianity by millennia, but since we're discussing Sgt. Howie's experience of May Day on Summerisle, we'll focus on Christianity for the moment.

8.   Some of these holidays were also regional, and not celebrated universally. St. Walpurga is primarily celebrated in Germany. Walpurga may have been a pagan goddess (see chapter 2). There are well over a dozen saints commemorated on May 1.

9.   See https://web.archive.org/web/20120815142641/http://anglopolish.com/index.php/en/archive/29-polish-tradition/155-international-workers-day-may-day.

10.   Edward Woodward refused to wear the exaggerated codpiece (see Brown, 2000: 53), but whether it was due to personal scruples or whether it's because Howie would do no such thing isn't noted.

11.   The flashbacks, in the director's cut, come sequentially before Howie's trip to Summerisle, making them not technically flashbacks at all.

12.   This is a different angle for viewing Clover's (2015) idea of the "final girl" trope. From the perspective of Michael Myers all the teenagers in Laurie Strode's circle must die or be transformed. The same applies to *April Fool's Day* and *Midsommar*.

13.   Barefoot (2017) notes that what is cinematic trash depends on who's defining it.

14.   This is perhaps the fuel that made *Tim Burton's The Nightmare before Christmas* (Henry Selick, 1993) such a success—it managed to blend two very distinct holidays.

15.   One counter to this is that Lord Summerisle notes that the fruit wilted on the bough in 1972, which suggests Midsummer could've been used. Of course, sex while already pregnant doesn't ensure a safe delivery.

CHAPTER 4: THE HORROR OF THEOLOGY

It's difficult to imagine Freddie Krueger or Jason Voorhees discussing the motivations behind their serial murders in theological terms. (Pinhead, however, inches into this territory.) *The Wicker Man* stands out in having its suave villain and true believer Lord Summerisle explain not only why Sgt. Howie must die, but also the theological background to his sacrifice. This is quite rare in horror. *Midsommar* comes close to *The Wicker Man* in offering a theological rationale for its unconventional beliefs. With many victims, however, it lacks the focus on one man whose very life depends on grasping the theology of an entire island.

In an effort to tie all of the foregoing together, this chapter will necessarily repeat some of the observations made earlier to put them into a larger framework. Systematic theologies, after all, attempt to systematize the various bits and pieces found in their base texts.

Howie's first meeting with Lord Summerisle consists entirely of theological dialogue. First-time viewers, not knowing where the story is headed, likely don't consider just how odd this is. Howie expresses shock at seeing naked girls jumping over a fire, which leads Summerisle to explain parthenogenesis, then the theology of the old gods. This interview, which is the key to the movie, continues into a discussion of how pre-Christian religion was re-introduced on Summerisle, to good effect. In terms of plot, this meeting between two sources of "secular" authority sets up the conflict of the film as one between religious motivations. Even the tall, modernly attired Christopher Lee towers over the uniformed, clean-cut Edward Woodward, suggesting the laird's superiority. Summerisle's explanations are contemporary, although bearing very old roots. Howie's god had his chance but, in Summerisle's words, "blew it."

Prior to his visit to the laird, Howie questioned the gardener in the graveyard (a hidden religious conceit of the disciples asking the gardener the location of Jesus' tomb in the New Testament) about their burial practices. These he finds unacceptable in the shadow of a ruined church. The gardener treats Howie's questions with a bemused knowing. The mystery behind this religion rests in it being so utterly foreign within a larger culture steeped in Christianity. It's a serious shock to Howie to discover a completely different belief system exists even in a world where Christian missionaries have reached every corner.

Figure 10. Bemused; note the out-of-focus cross. © British Lion

The difference between the religions of Sgt. Howie and Lord Summerisle comes down to the source of authority. Howie's religion is handed down from experts who continually, week by week, instruct their followers in what to believe. Summerisle's religion is, however, homegrown. His grandfather re-instituted the religion already in place before his time on the island. What the folk believe constitutes the actual definition of religion, and here on Summerisle Sgt. Howie is completely outnumbered by true believers. The folk determine religion and its rules. With enough of them even the power of the West Highland Constabulary can't save the sole heretic on an island of the faithful. Howie's usual status of representing the religion believed by everyone has been reversed. The power of *The Wicker Man* derives from believers whose celebration of May Day, they feel, will save them from another failed crop.

HOLIDAY THEOLOGY

Perhaps what makes *The Wicker Man* so exceptional is the effort that was put into the open discussion of theology. Apart from *The Exorcist*, this kind of sustained engagement is rare in horror. While some modern viewers find *The Exorcist* laughable, it still has the ability to frighten, largely based not only on its religious sincerity, but on the explanation given for what's happening to Regan MacNeil (Linda Blair). The extended playing-out of diagnosing Regan's illness as a religious one calls for a deep knowledge of Catholicism being shared with viewers. Far more common is the treatment in films like *The Possession* (Ole Bornedal, 2012). Here an Orthodox Jewish exorcist has to explain the ritual to a gentile who has no idea what's going on. Discussion of beliefs is brief and on a "need to know" basis, as the movie builds the horror without thoroughly explaining the religious reasons behind it. In *The Wicker Man*, however, religious imagery is both woof and warp of the story, like in *The Exorcist*. This is a difficult mix to pull off.

Both *The Wicker Man* and *The Exorcist* were released in 1973. So was the film of the musical *Jesus Christ Superstar* (Norman Jewison). Religion was, despite usual social conventions, being discussed in public. The horror prelude, as mentioned above, was laid out in *Rosemary's Baby*. It's hardly conceivable that before the sixties religion could've been presented as the basis for horror. The counterculture changed not only how sex was viewed, but also religion. While *Rosemary's Baby* didn't go deeply into theology, *The Omen* followed the emerging pattern of creating horror out of religious belief. Men sitting at a cafe discussing the Bible was new in horror. A fresh avenue for fear beyond the conventional monster was being developed.

Of course, *Wicker Man*, unlike these three near contemporaries, derives its religious horror from a specific holiday. Two main sources are helpful in reconstructing the theology of Summerisle: May Day traditions and the dialogue between Lord Summerisle and Sgt. Howie upon their first meeting. Little is known of ancient celebrations of May Day apart from some vestiges, such as maypoles, that may still occasionally be found (covered in chapter 2). This leads to a fictional accounting for the holiday and its theology. It is remarkably coherent.

Since many people come by their religious outlooks partially aided by cinema, looking to the fictional world of Summerisle becomes a legitimate means of explaining May Day. Historically Beltane would've been quite different, of course, but the movie provides a believable narrative that makes use of what can be historically known while cinematically embellishing it.

As noted in chapter 2, extensive native documents regarding Celtic religion and its holidays don't exist until after the Christianization of the Celts. Literacy, which became necessary with book-based religions such as Judaism and Christianity, was rare in ancient times. Not only that, but communication over long distances—there was no telephone or telegraph, let alone an internet—took months and wasn't frequent. As far as we know Celtic religion didn't have any kind of chief priest such as a pope. Religion was much more a local affair (Green, 2011). We don't have great amounts of information about the Druids, the supposed priestly caste of the Celts. In fact, it's unlikely that they should be considered priests at all (Ellis, 2002; see especially his introduction).

Since the plan for *Wicker Man* was to create a film where the fear comes from an unknown religion, an internally coherent holiday had to be constructed based on the fragmentary evidence we have from ancient times, such as Julius Caesar's sole reference to a wicker man. The result couldn't strain credulity, so it had to use ancient ideas with modern filler.

With Judaism's written records, we have somewhat detailed descriptions of what the holidays represented. The theology of the holidays is clearly laid out. Although the Bible doesn't do the same for Christianity, production of written records spread, and we can reconstruct the origins of holidays such as Christmas and Easter with some degree of confidence. Their theology is clear—the birth and resurrection of Jesus and their significance as the "reason for the season." Concerning the Celts, while some Christians had an academic interest in pre-Christian holidays, the earlier religion was generally considered dangerous in that it might draw people back away from the "one true faith." Holidays, especially joyfully celebrated occasions, could entice people away from Christianity.

While several of the elements discussed in chapter 2 have some historical precedent, as far as can be determined they never came together the way the film shows. Some elements, such as the wicker man himself, are historically unlikely, but there wouldn't be much a movie without him! It's important to bear in mind that even a fictional tale contributes to the evolving tradition of May Day. The elements come from different periods of history (if they're historical at all) and are constructed to make a narrative about sacrifice. It all comes together in the theology of the holiday. What is the theology of Summerisle's May Day?

To explore this, we'll follow Sgt. Howie's initiation into it.

AT THE POST OFFICE

After his initial interview with the men at the harbor, Howie learns that May Morrison runs the post office on the high street. In keeping with British practice, post offices offer other services besides handling letters; in this case it's also a sweet shop. Two prominent images seem to attract Howie's attention, as the insert shot shows—young children made of cake and chocolate hares. The hare will reappear throughout the movie, and rather like the rabbit in *The Witch*, it has significance (Grafius, 2020: 58–59; see also Krzywinska, 2000: 85–86). In *Wicker Man* the hare partially serves the function of that other famous springtime leporid, the Easter Bunny. Rabbits, and in this case hares, are symbols of life after death. Suddenly appearing in great numbers in the spring, they represent the renewal of life following the death of winter. They also represent fertility, which is essential to the religion of Summerisle. Myrtle Morrison declares that Rowan is a hare.

A twelve-year-old girl on the cusp of biological fertility is the typical May Queen, as the photographs on the wall of the Green Man reveal. Their burgeoning fertility encourages that of the crops on the island. The belief that like produces like lies behind much of what is termed "sympathetic magic," as noted above. While the villagers insist there is no Rowan Morrison, or they don't know how she died, Howie finds a hare in her coffin. Miss Rose notes that it's a fine transformation, another aspect of Howie's "fake biology." The theology here, while only part of the trap—Rowan is alive and well—involves the transmigration of souls. The islanders believe the dead (a word they don't use) transform. Howie's Christianity firmly rejects reincarnation, and the hare, already from the beginning, convinces him that the theology here is all wrong. The hare's supernatural associations (Krzywinska, 2000: 86), along with the mixing of human and animal, in Howie's religion create an inherently unholy combination.

The cakes shaped like children, one of which reappears later as May Morrison is slicing it when Howie enters to warn her that Rowan is to be sacrificed on May Day, are also a potent symbol. Not only have human likenesses served in various capacities in world religions, the concept of eating flesh is a distinct, distorted reflection of Howie's faith. Early Christians were sometimes accused of cannibalism due to the Eucharistic words "this is my body" (Wagemakers, 2010: 339–41). Interestingly, the prohibition against eating human flesh is never explicitly made in the Bible. A question remains regarding whether human sacrifice was practiced or not. Why should the Bible prohibit it if it didn't? It is, nevertheless, forbidden.

Figure 11. Human sacrifice clue. © British Lion

Already early in the film, the hints of human sacrifice appear. Even before we see the cake being cut, it is evident that the confectionary child is for eating. The cake knife May uses in the latter scene is quite large, overkill for a cake this size. Clues surround the detective, but he doesn't see.

SCHOOL AND GRAVEYARD

Howie's first lesson is sex education, which was the topic of chapter 3. Although he passed (or failed) the test with Willow, the topic is one that pervades both the film and the theology of Summerisle. Sex becomes intertwined with sacrifice. The next morning Willow first introduces the idea of May Day. Howie decides to visit the school to find clues about Rowan. Instead, clues of what the islanders believe point toward his own fate.

His first encounter is with the maypole. Historically, as noted in chapter 2, the maypole isn't a phallic symbol, but the islanders believe that it is. Remember, the belief of the folk constitutes religion. In the religion of Summerisle, May Day is about regeneration, reproduction. Miss Rose says as much directly, even as the Schoolmaster's song implies it. The fact that it's out in the open offends Sgt. Howie's Christian mores. His religion tries to separate adolescents from their naturally growing interest in sex. Tied with ribbons, the boys wind around the maypole. The maypole participates in a theology both of sex and of sacrifice.

The consistent pagan perspective of the islanders is complicated somewhat by a fleeting, peculiar camera angle during the maypole dance. The Schoolmaster sings about regeneration as the boys dance. Toward the end of the scene an insert shot presents his shadow on the ground, superimposed on that of the pole. He spreads his arms, creating a shadow cross. Perhaps this is less of a Christian symbol here than it is an indication that Howie will be sacrificed for his trust in that symbol. The theological message is reinforced in the schoolroom.

Figure 12. Shadow crucifix. © British Lion

Miss Rose tells the girls the maypole "is the image of the penis, which is venerated in religions such as ours as symbolizing the generative force in nature." Howie considers this the corruption of minors rather than theology. It is, however, essential to understanding May Day on Summerisle. Other aspects of their theology are spelled out on the blackboard, which Howie peremptorily erases. It lists the Snail Stone, the Toad Stone, and the Hag Stone (Howie is in the act of erasing the Cock-Knee Stone as the camera cuts from the girls to him) and their effects. These are borrowed from the New Age focus on stones and crystals. As for many New Age practices, some ancient precedent exists in the efficacy of certain types of stones (Blain, 2011: 1023–24). Theologically they point to the interconnectedness of nature, which is familiar from earth-centered religions.

When he opens Rowan's desk and finds the beetle winding around the nail—a perfect parallel to the maypole outside—Howie misses the symbolism of his own sacrifice.

When Daisy (Lesley Mackie) tells him that the beetle always goes the same way until trapped (just as Howie can't see their celebration for what it is), he asks in exasperation, "Then why in God's name do you do it, girl?" The answer to that question is all around—May Day's theology, if he were willing to learn it, would explain. It would save his life, but a sacrifice is necessary. Significantly, Miss Rose tells the girls to read from *The Rites and Rituals of May Day* as she takes a clueless Howie outdoors to talk.

Outside, Miss Rose explains their religion, which Howie simply dismisses. He asks if they've not heard of Christianity, unable to accept that they have and they've rejected it. She explains that they don't use the word "dead," believing instead that the soul returns in some form "to trees, to air, to fire, to water, to animals." Reincarnation involves regeneration, for which sex is generally necessary. Reincarnation is anathema to Christianity, of course. Howie can't believe anyone would reject the obvious truth of his own religion. Had he borrowed one of the schoolgirls' books, he would've learned, perhaps, that a May Day sacrifice is essential to this theology when crops fail.

Reincarnation will come up again in Howie's interview with Lord Summerisle, but it's worth pointing out that in the context of world religions it's an extremely common belief. Strands of both Buddhism and Hinduism accept as a matter of course that souls return after death in other forms. Christianity, seeing the event of Jesus' resurrection as singular and universal, simply cannot allow the return of souls. From the islanders' perspective, Howie's death will only be temporary.

Howie then visits the resting place of the rotting bodies. In the graveyard he sees a young mother breastfeeding her infant while holding an egg, as we've seen in chapter 2. The use of the egg symbol is similar to Christian Easter usage. An egg symbolizes rebirth. In Christianity it refers to Jesus, but to a nursing mother it suggests that life continues beyond death. Celts thought of death as birth into the Otherworld. Eggs, if the Roman historian Pliny the Elder is to be believed, were an important symbol in Celtic religion (Ellis, 2002: 60). Ironically, Howie brings sacrifice into the scene by fashioning a crude cross to place on one of the graves. He doesn't see, however, that he would be the victim of this sacrifice in the theology of someone else's religion.

Figure 13. Making religious conflict. © *British Lion*

Although the graveyard keeper doesn't directly address May Day in the next scene, he does explain that trees on graves are common practice. Trees in the popular imagination are connected with Druids, but again this isn't necessarily a May Day connection. This is followed by Howie's ride to visit Lord Summerisle. In the trap he sees the pregnant women blessing apple blossoms and Miss Rose's girls dancing naked around a fire in a stone circle. Both of these May Day activities help piece together the theology of the island. Summerisle explains the girls dancing in his first interview with the sergeant, but the blessing of the blossoms he doesn't mention. The apple trees are blossoming just as May is about to begin, situating it in the larger context of Beltane celebrations on Summerisle. They also symbolize regeneration.

The theology of *The Wicker Man* doesn't go beyond May Day. To turn that around, the reconstructed May Day of the movie is the basis of Summerisle's theology. Robin Hardy and Anthony Shaffer had researched "pagan" religions, and their Celtic religion was built around the celebration of May Day. Without the holiday there is no horror; May Day is for sacrifice. As Summerisle says, "We don't commit murder up here. We're a deeply religious people." He is, diegetically, sincere. From the theological view of the islanders, sacrifice can't be murder. What the gods demand is, by definition, moral. It derives from the fires of May Day.

To get at this theology we need to consider Howie's first interview with Summerisle in depth. Some of the lost footage, cut even before the film had been edited down to the theatrical version—it doesn't even appear in the director's cut—was a further explanation of this theology (Brown, 2000: 102–04). Since our focus here is the theatrical release we'll limit the discussion to what appears there rather than Shaffer's script. To get a better sense of the whole, however, it's helpful to know there was originally further material with which to work; the theology was thought through. We'll break it down thematically.

LORD SUMMERISLE ON REGENERATION

Sergeant Howie, still in shock from seeing the culturally tabooed naked dancing, is trying to figure out the unfamiliar—and to his mind licentious—behavior of the people on this island. Lord Summerisle hopes that the sight refreshes the policeman.

"It does not refresh me," Howie firmly replies. Summerisle expresses his regrets, noting that everyone should be open to "the regenerative influences." Notice he doesn't say "reproductive." Regenerative is a word that connotes, biologically, the growth of new bodily elements to replace those lost or damaged. Theologically, however, "regeneration" connotes spiritual rebirth.[1] In his choice of this word, Summerisle introduces the religious aspect of the sustainability of life. People live and grow through the regeneration of cells, but this can also be seen as a spiritual reality. Sex is clearly part of it. That seems to be how Summerisle looks at it. The Christian Howie, ironically, can't get beyond the physicality of it.

Naked girls imply immorality. Christianity has long had a discomfort with nudity. Part of it has to do with "temptation"—since sex is sinful, any temptation towards initiating sexual activity becomes immoral in its own right, except within very limited contexts of marriage. This idea is deeply rooted in western monotheistic culture; not all religious systems share it. Hinduism, for example, doesn't shy from representing naked goddesses and ithyphallic gods. In Christianity even suggesting such a thing is sacrilege. Believing only one religion can possibly be true, Howie considers this prohibition of nudity, at least publicly, to be absolute. He can't see it as part of any legitimate theology.[2]

Regeneration, however, also suggests society regrowing its lost or damaged parts. So Howie exhumes the coffin that night only to find a hare instead of a human. Confronting Summerisle and Miss Rose with his findings, he indicates that the substitution is mockery after Miss Rose comments, "Personally I think this makes a very lovely transmutation." Of course, she knows Rowan isn't really dead. This underscores the need for caution here. The May Day theology of Summerisle can be reconstructed, but the fact that it is also part of a massive deception must be kept in mind. Knowing that Howie is being trapped raises the question of the sincerity of the belief system. The fact that they are sacrificing him, however, suggests true belief.[3] We'll return to this sincerity point shortly.

Transmutation as a form of regeneration makes sense among people who don't discuss death. The island regenerates its population, somewhat like the house regenerates itself in *Burnt Offerings* (Dan Curtis, 1976). The population includes not just humans, but the animals and plants as well. Any one part might be regenerated and transmuted to a different part. The needs of the whole are met that way. Transmutation is tied to reincarnation; the soul returns, but not always in human form. Some Celtic traditions believed that souls of the dead could return in trees (Hutton, 2011: 11).

As noted, Christianity, with its belief in the uniqueness of the resurrection of Jesus, cannot support the idea of reincarnation. Indeed, it has been considered antithetical to Christian teaching from the beginning. The resurrected dead go on to eternal reward or punishment. There's no coming back. The religion expressed in this May Day celebration, as indicated by Miss Rose and the Schoolmaster, is one of constantly returning through the cycles of nature. Christianity proposes a single, unilinear set of unique events—a "salvation history" with a beginning, middle, and end. The cyclical nature of Summerisle's belief in regeneration completely dismantles this belief in a set of singular occurrences—it's a cycle. May Day is one point in that cycle. Regeneration can lead to eternity even as Christian thought promotes, only the endless cycle is in this world, not outside of it as in Christian concepts of eternity.

LORD SUMMERISLE ON PARTHENOGENESIS

Questioning Summerisle's claim that the islanders are deeply religious—ruined churches, no ministers—Howie comes back again to the real stumbling block of sexuality. Children dancing naked around a fire simply offends his Christian prudishness. He sees no possible religious lesson they could learn from it. Lord Summerisle attempts to explain parthenogenesis, but is quickly cut off by Howie's "fake biology" objection. What is parthenogenesis and was it Celtic?

Parthenogenesis comes from two Greek words, one for virgin (*parthen*) and one for origin (*genesis*), thus "origin from a virgin" translates the idea well. It seems to be an extremely ancient concept. Myths going all the way back to Mesopotamia present scenarios where gods, of either gender, generate children alone, thus "reproduction without sexual union." Instead of rushing to fake biology, it's worth noting that understanding the mechanisms of reproduction is recent, and scientific. (Ironically Howie's religion, that so often conflicts with science, here relies on it.) Not all ancient peoples recognized that sex was necessary for reproduction, although the cause and consequence of this was obvious to most. Not understanding ovum and sperm—both are too small to see without a microscope—ancients had varying ideas about how this worked technically. In such a worldview parthenogenesis wasn't too much to ask, even if it was very rare.

Howie might've more productively challenged Summerisle on why the islanders sleep around, then. Why had Willow just the night before invited him to have sex? Here we come up against Occam's Razor. The idea of Occam's Razor is basically that if one explanation is sufficient then further explanations are superfluous. This concept has a valued place in scientific thinking, but religions often accept multiple explanations for rites and rituals. Although religious thinking can be precise and analytical, it is more often vague and mysterious. So on this island girls would be thrilled to be divinely impregnated. Of course, the old-fashioned way comes with its own benefits. Either way the end result is fertility, regeneration.

Did the Celts believe in parthenogenesis? Unfortunately we don't have detailed descriptions of Celtic mythology before Christianization was well underway. We simply don't know the answer to that question. It would not be unlikely that such a belief occurred in Celtic cultures, but we don't have any way of knowing. Many ancient religions held some kind of belief in parthenogenesis. The words of the girls' song about the fire seed confirm that, diegetically at least, the belief is well incorporated on Summerisle.

This clash of worldviews is brought on by the strongly sexualized element to it. Remember, as we saw in chapter 3, Christianity has strict rules concerning sex. This makes Summerisle's rebuff that Jesus was "the son of a virgin, impregnated, I believe, by a ghost," one of the few moments Howie is at a loss for words in the film. As Summerisle explains more precisely, it leads to his main point. The old gods aren't dead.

THE OLD GODS

Sergeant Howie's theology is completely entangled with the Christian opportunistic engagement with science. Turned the other way around, western science developed within a distinctly Christian worldview. In western culture the earliest scientific thinkers were all products of a thoroughly Christianized Europe (whether or not they were Christian). Some, such as Sir Isaac Newton, were actively religious (in his own way), while others, such as Galileo, likely accepted Catholicism as granted. At least as far as the basic history of salvation goes. Science grew from the worldview of monotheism with a deliberately created universe. God may have taken a back seat after he set it in motion but there was no questioning the divinity of Jesus and the efficacy of his resurrection, for the most part.

This is highlighted when Lord Summerisle tells Howie that on this island the old gods are not dead. Christianity had multiple ways of dealing with the old gods. One was simply to poke fun at them as mere idols—this even occurred as early as the Hebrew Bible. Another way of dealing with them was to claim they were in fact demons who set out to deceive gullible pre-Christians. Yet another method was to make the gods into saints and say that they were actually super-Christians. No matter how they were handled, it was clear that the old gods were a problem for monotheism. Not only did people have a long-standing belief in them, they also managed to remain in place even after conversion.

Believing the old gods merely myths, Howie gives a typical retort: "What of the true God?" The question more than implies; it proclaims directly that any other gods are false. There can be no dialogue if Howie remains convinced of his own orthodoxy and refuses to consider Summerisle's point of view.

Let's examine the scene closely. When Summerisle tells him that the Christian God "blew it," Howie stands bolt erect in military posture. He has gone into combat mode, a status he'd been quite near already. His "What?!" is part question and part threat. Already determined to bring the wrath of God down on these pagans, his religion betrays its fragility at the first real challenge it has perhaps ever faced in the context of a "Christian country."

But who are these old gods? Counts of ancient Celtic deities vary, with over 300 being named. The central pantheon of deities, however, seems to have numbered 33 (Ellis, 2002: 114; see also Green, 2011). *Wicker Man* doesn't make too much of the specifics. The names of two gods only are mentioned, and these during the preparations for the May Day celebration: Nuada and Avellenau. Summerisle also invokes "the god of the sea," but doesn't name him. Celtic gods were written about only after Roman incursions, and their mythology has to be reconstructed. Neither Nuada nor Avellenau are among the most prominent deities (Green, 2011), but in Summerisle's May Day they reign. The two named deities are especially appropriate to May Day, controlling as they do the sun (Nuada) and orchards (Avellenau).

The possibility of the old gods still existing appears in other horror films as well, such as the offbeat *Cabin in the Woods*. What drives *Wicker Man*, however, isn't the reality of those deities, but the belief in their reality. The film's fear derives from what religiously motivated people might do in a holiday mood if no outside authority is watching. There's no real reason to doubt the sincerity of that belief, for that is precisely the engine of the horror.

We've left Sgt. Howie standing. What follows is the full explanation behind the May Day celebration that will take place the next day, leading to his death.

THE LAIRD EXPLAINS

In the calm manner that makes him such a perfect villain, Summerisle reveals to Howie what's behind the veil. Summerisle's grandfather, a Victorian scientist, bought the island to carry out agricultural experiments. The locals, under the care of their Christian ministers, had been starving. To an agronomist's eyes there was no reason for this. Rich volcanic soil warmed by the Gulf Stream should allow for hardy crops even in Scotland. The first Lord Summerisle required the labor of the islanders to make his experiments succeed. His problem was how to motivate them. He hit upon a solution that continues to work even today—he made the motivation religious.

Giving back their "joyous old gods" says volumes about the centuries of Christian control. First of all, it says the people never forgot their ancestral beliefs. Christian missionaries had relentlessly converted them from a happy paganism to a dour Presbyterianism (if we take the viewpoint of history—Howie is an Anglican, a minority form of Christianity in Scotland). Historical descriptions of the practice of a harsh Reform religion demonstrate viable reasons for unhappiness. Calvinism is a strict, stripped-down form of Christianity. No ceremony, no color, no joy. It teaches predestination—the belief that God has pre-decided who will be saved and who will be damned. Nothing you can do will change that. This is the religion that motivates the family in Robert Eggers' The Witch (Grafius, 2020). While theologians can offer reasons to live a good life, the average person is left in fear, never knowing if they'll make the cut or not.

The first Lord Summerisle knew that the Celtic celebrations were more enjoyable. The May Day religion constructed for Wicker Man includes free sexuality—he was a "free thinker"—dancing, singing, drinking, and rowdy behavior. These are exactly the kinds of things Calvinism suppresses. By the way, free-thinking religious groups have historically existed from time to time. The Oneida Community of John Humphrey Noyes (1811–86) was founded roughly the same time as Summerisle's fictional grandfather, in upstate New York. It practiced "communal marriage," although its religion was more contemplative than the Celtic paganism imagined by The Wicker Man (Carden, 1998). Singing and dancing and what we might call "partying" were strictly repressed by the Presbyterianism that overtook Scotland in the wake of John Knox. Giving the people back a religion that motivates by carrot rather than stick demonstrates that the original laird recognized that people needed holidays.

Summerisle reveals that what his grandfather in reality did was to develop strains of fruit suitable to the climate while giving credit to the old gods. There's reason for some cynicism here, since Summerisle knows the truth behind the success of this agricultural experiment. There is a scientific explanation. The islanders responded to their new-found prosperity by giving credit to the old gods—after all, if your god leaves you starving and in poverty, the non-theologian sees that something must be wrong. Over time they came to believe it really was the old gods who blessed them for returning to the native religion of the region.

Interestingly, Summerisle notes that the Christian ministers fled the island when the efficacy of the "miraculous" thriving of the trees became evident. Religious tests such as this are common in the Bible, with, of course, the biblical deity always winning. A "miracle" demonstrates a power that forces acknowledgment of a superior god. The Christian clergy realized they couldn't win against what was really science, but what the islanders believed in was divine help. With Christianity absent, the restored old-time religion was the only belief system on the island.

This scenario had been devised out of "expediency," as Summerisle notes. His own father, however, continued it because of love. Love is a strong motivator when it comes to religion. While not exactly the same as belief, it implies the sincere acceptance of the old gods. Parents in any belief system want their children to thrive by teaching them the true religion. In this case his father taught him "to reverence the music and the drama and the rituals of the old gods," even while knowing that his own father had reinstated the religion for more practical purposes. Summerisle provides a kind of creed with which he was raised—to love and fear nature, and, more ominously, to appease it. Appeasement brings the dialogue back to its starting point—sacrifice. Howie misreads this as the sacrifice of Rowan, as the islanders intend for him to do. Howie sees Scotland as a Christian nation.

CHRISTIAN NATIONALISM

The culture wars of the past several decades have often centered around the idea that European and North American nations were founded as Christian. The reasoning goes that if that's how they were established, then religion is the pillar upon which the nations stand. Self-identity coalesces around a religious system. The United Kingdom, where Sgt. Howie resides, has a long pagan prehistory. His warning to Lord Summerisle that he is a subject of a "Christian country" reflects the lawful interpretation of the religious conflicts that pepper the history of the nation.

Howie's appeal to the law can see only a Protestant Britain, ignoring the long and violent Christian conflict between Protestant and Catholic. Christian, for him, means civilized, despite the evidence of history. Throughout the movie Howie is portrayed as not a particularly deep thinker. His understanding of history is limited, and his sense of ethical correctness fits only a narrow view of what Christianity is. He seems unaware that his own Anglicanism is the historic result of conflict with Roman Catholicism. Indeed, he glosses over the fact that most of Scotland is Presbyterian, a belief system in conflict with his own. His assessment of Summerisle's religion is that it can be dismissed with the disparaging word "pagan." An inferior and debased religion.

The initial interview with Summerisle ends with Howie's accusation of "pagan" hanging in the air. That night, after exhuming Rowan's body and finding a hare, he returns to Summerisle to confront him with the fact. When Summerisle asks him what he thinks might've happened, Howie, barely containing his anger, declares, "I think Rowan Morrison was murdered, under circumstances of pagan barbarity, which I can scarcely bring myself to believe is taking place in the twentieth century." Did you catch it? "Pagan" is used as a dismissive slur from the perspective of a superior religion. Pagans are barbarous, ignoring the long—and continuing—violence between Protestants and Catholics where barbarity was, and sometimes still is, common.

State-sponsored religion is nearly as old as organized religion. As noted, early in human society the monarchy supported the priesthood and the priesthood supported the monarchy. As two bases of power in society they were separate but closely related. Each had a vested interest in the power and success of the other. That model has prevailed throughout history, even if it's unofficial. In Britain the monarch is the head of the Church of England. What Howie overlooks, however, is that that fact doesn't mandate everyone be Christian, or even Church of England members (such as he himself is, by extension at least). By the 1970s the power of the Church over secular matters of law had already diminished. The country may be Christian in name, but that isn't the same as being so in practice.

Summerisle ends his official encounters with Howie the same way that Willow MacGregor ended his wake-up call. He tells Howie he'll not want to be on the island to witness their May Day celebration. Remember, this is holiday horror. The theological talk is a slow build to how May Day is celebrated after a failed harvest, culminating in sacrifice.

SACRIFICE

The first-time viewer doesn't realize how everything happening to Howie is a test to see if he's the perfect sacrifice. While there's no historical evidence associating it with Beltane, the concept of sacrifice is one that has ancient roots in pre-Christian religion. Christianity grew out of Judaism, which, according to the Bible, had a vibrant sacrificial cult (remember, "cult" means the practice of religion). Daily animal sacrifices along with occasional sacrifices kept the temple staff well fed. Indeed, sacrifices were a regular expectation for holidays. Christianity understood the human, or more theologically correct human/divine, sacrifice of Jesus to be a culmination of the sacrificial system. Jesus died, the thinking goes, so that nobody else has to pay the penalty for sins. Theologians have explored various interpretations of the reasons for this, but it made sense given that the Hebrew Bible—the Bible of early Christians—emphasized the sacrificial system. The breakdown of that system at the destruction of the Temple was a sign of God's wrath.

Ironically, Judaism inherited its ideas of sacrifice from earlier, polytheistic religions. As archaeologists explored the lands surrounding ancient Israel, they discovered many pre-biblical texts. One thing made abundantly clear from these texts is that sacrifice wasn't something first revealed to Moses; it was a way of life well established among the "heathen." Judaism may have adjusted the theology behind it to fit a monotheistic outlook, but the basic practice was pagan. Everywhere people seem to have had the idea that gods demand death. On its most practical level—Sgt. Howie will be an exception here—the sacrificial system helps absolve the guilt people feel about slaughtering animals for food. Pagan cultures around the world that still rely on hunting commonly thank the animal for giving its life for the humans who eat it.

Ancient Egyptians, Mesopotamians, and Syrians—all of Israel's neighbors—had sacrificial systems. Sacrifice helped support the temple staff and benefited the royal household as well. A stable society grew out of a monarchy supported by a priesthood and a priesthood supported by a monarchy. Summerisle has its laird. Making this the will of the gods ensured nobody would question why they had to give up their precious animals to support the state. Judaism transformed these into divine commandments of the one God.

It can't be denied that Christianity is based on a singular human sacrifice. Many early Christians emulated that sacrifice, deliberately putting themselves in the way of authorities so that they would be killed (Moss, 2014). So it is that Lord Summerisle can tell the trapped Sgt. Howie, after he proclaims that he believes in eternal life, "That is good. For believing what you do, we confer upon you a rare gift these days—a martyr's death."

Some slight evidence of holiday sacrifices may be hinted at in the feasting that is historically attested on May Day. In societies prior to the advent of grocery stores, feasts generally meant slaughter, and slaughter with a religious rationale is sacrifice. Even if so, sacrifice isn't attested as a major feature of Beltane (Hutton, 1996: 226–43). *The Wicker Man* doesn't portray feasting, but it most definitely has a May Day sacrifice.

The crops failed, Howie will desperately try to explain, because the soil doesn't support the strains of crops they grow. There's something unnatural about palm trees growing in the Hebrides.[4] "That's why your crops failed," he shouts. Ironically, it was Lord Summerisle who explained this to him in their interview. Many hints of sacrifice occur before the wicker man himself appears. As the procession makes its way into the stone circle, Summerisle carries a sickle. At the circle the chop game feigns a beheading. Axing a cask of ale to offer it to the god of the sea is another sacrifice. It's written all over Summerisle's May Day.

THE RIGHT KIND OF SACRIFICE

Any sacrifice after that of Jesus is murder, from Howie's point of view. In Summerisle's view the trap set for Howie isn't murder, it's sacrifice. When Howie realizes that he is to be killed, just before being placed in the wicker man, he tells the people "you can wrap it up any way you like; you are about to commit murder." They all begin humming to cover his words, just like true believers. Sacrifice, like "capital punishment," isn't murder. A divinely required death is a moral obligation rather than an immoral murder. This distinction can only be seen through the eyes of religious belief. The theology of Summerisle prevents this from being murder.

Anthony Shaffer, in an interview on *The Wicker Man Enigma* documentary, stated that the movie is about sacrifice. Historically the practice of animal sacrifice was psychologically disturbing. Ritual was built around it and the guilt of taking an innocent life was covered over by a divine requirement. *Wicker Man* asks, if it worked with animals back then, might it work with human beings even now?

This theme is woven throughout the movie. On May Day itself—the day of sacrifice—a frantic Sgt. Howie bursts into May Morrison's shop to try to persuade her to reveal where her daughter is. She is cutting the humanoid cake with apparent unconcern as she tells Howie he'll never understand the true nature of sacrifice. The double significance here, of course, is that he is the unknowing sacrifice. Summerisle will later explain his role in it.

The core concept of sacrifice is appeasement. Gods are capable of making human life easy or difficult. To sway them toward making life better for humanity, people must give the gods gifts. As Summerisle explains to Howie as he's about to be placed in the eponymous wicker man, animals have limited effectiveness, and although a child works, the best sacrifice is the right kind of adult. The right kind of adult—and this is simply fabricated for the film—has four qualities: willingness, kingship, virginity, and foolishness. Let's examine each.

Willingness, in the case of animals, is impossible to determine. As far as human sacrifice goes, willingness isn't historically a requirement. The needs of a society outweigh the needs of an individual. In Howie's case, however, his willingness is questionable. One of the elements of David Pinner's book that carries over has to do with just this point— Lord Summerisle says they controlled Howie's thoughts since he arrived. In *Ritual* the witches practice mind control on David Hanlin. At points in *Wicker Man*, Howie's actions do seem to be too much in line with the islanders' plans, for example when he reads the library book about the rituals they observe. Could he have found that exact book without their prompting? Is he willing? Since we never see the results of his death we simply can't know if it was effective.

Kingship, as noted in chapter 2, involves Howie being a police officer, a representative of the king. Howie completely identifies with this. As he tells Lord Summerisle, "I'm interested in one thing—the law." Howie reminds Summerisle of his being a citizen of a Christian country. In his eyes, Howie's authority, and that authority structure, is absolute.

Virginity was discussed in chapter 3. Young animals—before sexual maturity—were sometimes mandated for biblical sacrifices. Giving up an individual who hasn't realized their reproductive potential is a sign that the gods should take this offering sincerely. It's especially valuable because it sacrifices regeneration through sexual means.

Foolishness, discussed in chapter 2, isn't so much a sacrificial requirement as it is a psychological one. Apart from someone believing they could get away with being king for a day with no consequences, who would be willing to do it? In Summerisle theology, a foolish, willing, virgin who was king encapsulates all the things they seem not to have in their own population.

While it's not specified in Celtic tradition that such a sacrifice occurs on May Day, generally sacrificial religions do provide specific regulations about what kind of sacrifice is acceptable. Sometimes extensive requirements apply. In this holiday horror, Sgt. Howie is tailor-made for May Day's sacrifice on Summerisle.

DANGEROUS HOLIDAYS

Why don't we work every single day? Most people don't stop to think that time off work—holidays and vacations—are religious innovations. No written records of the earliest practiced holidays survive, but it seems clear that observances of changes in seasons or portentous events were originally associated with the gods. By the time we have coherently explained narrative rationales for holidays in the Bible—the basis for much of western civilization—the reasons are explicitly religious.

Not only that, but the idea of taking a weekly day off work, the beginning of the weekend concept, was also biblical, as we've seen. The idea behind the Sabbath was theological. The idea of subsistence laborers with animals to care for taking a day off was likely never a reality. A day off work benefited those in more urban environments. Nevertheless, the groundwork for our weekend—the holiday that occurs weekly—is religious. While there are also civil holidays, in ancient times there was no part of life that didn't involve religion.

May Day, as we considered in depth in chapter 2, is a religious holiday. The fact that it no longer garners a great deal of attention only adds to the sense of foreignness or disorientation Sgt. Howie feels on Summerisle—he doesn't have any substantial experience of the holiday. He doesn't know how it's celebrated by true believers. Not only that, but time set off from the workaday world is liminal time.

The concept of liminal time relates to crossing a threshold. In a theological sense it refers to entering sacred time instead of secular time. It isn't always safe to do so. Much of modern religion, at least viewed in popular perception, believes that sacred time is upright, wholesome, and safe. Ancient religious thought didn't hold to these standards. Religion is what the gods demand, whether it seems right to humans or not.[5] Religious demands may not be "family friendly." And religion certainly isn't always safe. The religion of Summerisle has this in common with Christianity—religion is a matter of following what the divine demands, no matter how uncomfortable.

The sacred nature of holidays puts them into dangerous territory. The classic study of the sacred is a 1917 book by a German Lutheran theologian named Rudolf Otto (1869–1937). In his book, *The Idea of the Holy*, he describes the numinous nature of religious experience. The holy is what he describes with the Latin words *mysterium tremendum et fascinans*, a mystery that terrifies yet fascinates. Although people are drawn to it, it also frightens them precisely because it's dangerous. This concept lies behind much of horror that involves religious themes. Think of classics such as *Rosemary's Baby*, *The Exorcist*, or *The Omen*. Or even the second member of the folk horror unholy trinity, *The Blood on Satan's Claw*. Religion itself is scary as well as compelling. Otto's time-honored ideas play right into horror and religion. Since holidays generally have religious origins (how many horror films are made about Labor Day or Summer Bank Holiday?), holiday horror often covers this ground.

Just because something is sacred doesn't mean it's safe. May Day demonstrates just how this works in *Wicker Man*'s reconstruction of a holiday. Normally it's a joyous celebration with bountiful harvests demonstrating the pleasure of Nuada and Avellenau. The Green Man's sequence of pre-1972 photos demonstrates this. Only the intentionally missing 1972 image clues Howie into the more savage demands that a failed crop requires, the dangerous side of religious holidays. The side that requires the ultimate sacrifice.

Figure 14. The wicker man. © British Lion

The Celts, like most ancient peoples, probably practiced human sacrifice rarely. Keeping in mind that most of our records are from outside—and often judgmental—sources, archaeology supports that it occasionally happened (Cunliffe, 1997; Ellis, 2002; Hutton, 2009; Green, 2011). The evidence for using a wicker man to do so goes back to a single source, Posidonius, picked up and made standard by Julius Caesar. Historians doubt that it ever really took place. It certainly had no place in regular May Day rituals. The film requires it, however. Religion can lead to horror if it falls on the right holiday.

Theologically the wicker man fits the world of the movie perfectly. *Wicker Man* is not just about sacrifice but human sacrifice. Howie, an intelligent if too opinionated man, is fully aware of what he's about to undergo once the wicker man is revealed. The horror on his face at that moment is the culmination of holiday horror—socially sanctioned death based on a religion that has a coherent system demanding it. A day set aside for propitiating the gods, a role that in Christianity was sloughed off on Jesus of Nazareth.[6] The horror comes from the uncompromising nature of the holiday. Someone had to be sacrificed, and the religion on Summerisle dictates that it must be a certain kind of stranger.

Many religions, including that which Howie believes, protect the stranger. The sympathies of the viewer of *The Wicker Man* are clearly with Howie, alone, unarmed, and incapable of reasoning with true believers. It's fitting at this point to return to Robin Hardy's statement that this is a cautionary tale. The caution isn't restricted to what are popularly called cults,[7] but to any religion that's taken too seriously. Reports of holiday excesses are generally followed by expressions of regret, of being carried away with the moment. That may be required for something as extreme as human sacrifice.

Our everyday, rational approach toward life in society militates against frequently getting carried away to such a point. Even evolutionary ethics make same-species killings rare. Humans know this is a very serious matter. A theology that becomes so potent as to overturn this deeply ingrained morality is something to be feared. *The Wicker Man* cautions against taking a religious holiday too seriously. Even Christianity is founded on a theology of human sacrifice as the basis for a springtime holiday that forms an acceptable version of horror to propitiate the demand of a deity for sacrifice in order to wipe out sin.

NOTES

1. The *Oxford English Dictionary*. Certainly in Christian theology it has that connotation.
2. This same moralism is reflected in Ingham (2018: 33–42).
3. Religions, as they develop, evolve religious specialists who come to know that contradictions, inconsistencies, and inaccuracies exist in the usual beliefs of the laity. Not all Christians attend seminary, for example, to grapple with these difficulties. It doesn't mean they are any less sincere for it. *Wicker Man* presents an informed practitioner in the form of Lord Summerisle. Howie would discover his own faith has inconsistencies as well, were he to undertake advanced religious training.
4. Palm trees actually do grow in some of the Scottish islands, such as Arran. The Gulf Stream circulates relatively warm ocean water through the North Channel, making parts of the North Atlantic region conducive to semi-tropical plants. This is not fiction in *The Wicker Man*.
5. In the Bible, God orders Abraham to kill his son Isaac. Even though this is a test, as we later find out, the demand itself is wrong.
6. It could be argued that *The Passion of the Christ* (2004) is a horror film, focusing as it does on the bodily and spiritual suffering of Jesus, in Mel Gibson's vision of his final days.

7. Religion scholars use the word "cult" quite differently and prefer the term New Religious Movements for what are titled cults in the media.

CONCLUSION: CONFLICT AND LEGACY

As with any piece of true art, much about *The Wicker Man* is open to dispute. Which version is definitive? Whose recollections are accurate as to whether this or that happened?[1] How much of the story was borrowed from David Pinner's *Ritual*? Or the higher-level questions—what does the film mean? Who has the right to say? The director? The writer? The producer? The actors? (Many academics have come to view the viewers' interpretations as equally as valid as those of the creators.) The fact that an entire book could be dedicated to trying to sort this out (Allan Brown's *Inside* The Wicker Man) should be an indication that any book on the movie will be met with disagreement among those who already have opinions on several aspects of the film and its history and impact.

At this point Robin Hardy, Anthony Shaffer, Christopher Lee, Edward Woodward, Diane Cilento, Ingrid Pitt, and even Lindsay Kemp, Aubrey Morris, and Walter Carr are dead. The afterlife of the film and its treatment by British Lion, especially after the company's acquisition by Barclay Securities, are well documented. Other books and articles treat this in detail (Bartholomew, 1977; Brown, 2000), but the basics run like this.

British Lion, the production and distribution company that was backing *Wicker Man*, underwent a change of leadership near the final stages of the movie. The 102-minute version now known as "The Director's Cut" was cut by about 14 minutes, giving us the original release version (88 minutes) that is the basis of this book. A third version, with some restored material but not all of it, titled "The Final Cut," was released in 2013. All three versions are available for those diligent enough to seek them out. When Robin Hardy went back to British Lion for the original, uncut, negatives, plus the outtakes, he was informed that the originals had been lost. There is the suggestion that they were accidentally sent to be used as motorway fill. Versions of the director's cut have rough transitions where scenes that were re-shot from the positive print have been integrated into the original release. To make matters even more complicated, "The Final Cut," which is 92 minutes versus the original 88, claims by its very title to be the last word. There is no last word about *The Wicker Man*.

Each of the three differs in ways that affect reconstructing the story. Since the original release has had the longest availability to the viewing public, and is the basis for the initial cult following for the film, it is the version used for this book. (Obviously, adding another night on Summerisle or changing when Willow propositions Howie changes things.) Other writers on the film have documented that further additional scenes were shot and survive in a few stills, but these are mostly gone forever.

In the face of all this misfortune, *The Wicker Man* has nevertheless been recognized as one of the great British film efforts of the 1970s, and it has gained a tremendous fan base since then. More than that, however, it was one of the early movies of the holiday horror sub-genre. What exactly happened in the making of the film? Conflicting memories and alternative narratives will never be able to be reconciled. We can, however, appreciate this gem of a movie even in a truncated—one might be tempted to say castrated—version. The story is cohesive and quirky. More than that, it left a legacy.

The story of *The Wicker Man*'s distribution problems is legendary. British Lion, under the leadership of producer Peter Snell, was sold during the filming process, and EMI's transition team, on behalf of the new owner, wasn't at all thrilled about this particular movie (Brown, 2000; Murray and Rolston, 2008). Despite its torturous route to distribution and initial lackluster response, it eventually became a cult classic. Cinderella stories such as this often attract directors and producers who imagine how a film might have been better made. Reboots are nothing unusual. In fact, Hardy and Lee had been considering this as well, once the original proved somewhat successful (Bing, 2002).

LEGACY

Anthony Shaffer and Robin Hardy had a falling-out after *The Wicker Man*. Each went his own way in attempting to build a franchise around it. Shaffer left a screenplay for *The Loathsome Lambton Worm*, a proper sequel to *The Wicker Man*. To date it hasn't been produced, although the manuscript has been available since 1989. Hardy began work on his own continuation of the story that eventually became *The Wicker Tree* (2011). But first, fans had to endure a reboot set in America, released in 2006.

The rights for the remake went to Universal (at the time, eventually Warner Brothers), and Neil LaBute became the writer and director. Turning back to David Pinner's *Ritual*, rather than Frazer's *Golden Bough* or the work of Joseph Campbell that had helped propel *Star Wars* to intergalactic success, LaBute changed the setting, the basic premise, and, most importantly, nearly left May Day out of it. In fact, religion in the reboot is understated to the point of near irrelevance. What Hardy and Shaffer understood—religion drives the fear in the movie—was ignored, and the remake was critically burnt in its own wicker man.

Briefly: Edward Malus (Nicolas Cage) is a tortured police officer. His ex-fiancée Willow (Kate Beahan) has gone home to re-join a band of female neo-pagans (who are portrayed somewhat negatively, as in the novel) on the island of SummersIsle off the coast of Washington. Her daughter Rowan is missing. As in the original, the islanders have set Malus up and lead him on a frantic search for Rowan, who, it turns out, is his daughter also. (No virgin he.) The islanders support themselves through honey production. Since it has failed they need a human sacrifice, and Edward is the chosen one.

Despite some clever re-use of names and nods to the original (Malus is Latin for "apple," his first name Edward and Willow's surname Woodward are based on the original Howie, and so forth), the remake misses the horror suggested by ancient rites practiced in isolation. The religion of the neo-pagan women isn't historical in any sense, and although it can kill there's no inherent religious threat in it. Fear of undiscovered Druids and what they might be up to is quite a different proposition. LaBute's remake tried to center the horror in the basic story outline, but leaving out archaic May Day rites—untenable in any "neo" religion—took the fuel from the fire.

On Hardy's Summerisle the people firmly and unquestioningly believe the old religion. A firmly believed religion and a pagan holiday far from the "civilized" Christian world suggest something horrible may happen. Lord Summerisle knows the history of his religion; he explains it in plain terms to Sgt. Howie (while leaving some facts omitted, of course). The people, the folk, however, believe it to be true. On the SummersIsle of the 2006 version, a further problematic backstory is added. The women of this neo-pagan religion fled England to settle in Salem. Although common enough in horror (H. P. Lovecraft was fond of using Salem to indicate actual witchery), the suggestion that the women and men of Salem were actually participating in practices that were diabolical defames the memory of innocent women (mostly) who were executed due to religious hysteria. This is exactly the kind of history that requires a cautionary tale. The remake, however, simply uses Salem as a convenient cultural stopping point to an island of women and their mysterious beliefs. Why honey? What ancient religion was based on beekeeping? On Summerisle May Day is celebrated with deadly seriousness. The viewer has to believe that or the story falls apart. The belief reaches as far as murder.

It is tempting to think that Robin Hardy decided to pursue *The Wicker Tree* because of this poorly made reboot, but Hardy wrote *Cowboys for Christ*, the novel on which the film was based, after attempting to find support for a new movie in the franchise. The novel was published in 2006, the year LaBute's remake was released. Hardy had pitched his idea even earlier, which suggests that the desire to franchise *The Wicker Man* predated the actual remake.

A number of familiar names reappear in *The Wicker Tree*. British Lion was again among the production companies, and Peter Snell was one of the producers. The film has some of the quirkiness of the original, but takes the story on a long and somewhat convoluted journey. Two American missionaries, Beth Boothby (Brittania Nicol) and Steve Thompson (Henry Garrett), members of Cowboys for Christ, are sent to Scotland to convert the pagans. Engaged, they abstain from sex and wear chastity rings. They meet Sir Lachlan Morrison (Graham McTavish) and his wife Lady Delia (Jacqueline Leonard) and learn they have sponsored one of their concerts (Beth is the more prominent of the two missionaries because she sings). The name "Morrison" suggests, of course, May Morrison and daughters from *The Wicker Man*. Sir Lachlan runs the Nuada nuclear power plant in Tressock, in the Scottish Borders region. The mainland location, particularly in the relatively accessible lowlands, translates to a less isolated setting that nevertheless plays into folk horror. At Tressock Beth and Steve have "success" at winning over some locals who worship the goddess Sulis, a Celtic sun goddess. The locals invite the missionaries to stay for May Day, making this also holiday horror. The holiday isn't foregrounded as in *The Wicker Man*, and that may be part of the problem.

For unexplained reasons—there seems to be no history behind any of this—the people of Tressock stuff and preserve their May Queens, and they have targeted Beth. Likewise, with no explanations, they have a "laddie" crown the May Queen, although this is actually a ruse. Steve is the laddie, and he is ripped apart by the pagans and eaten. They do this to restore their fertility, which has been destroyed by the nuclear power plant. Before being consumed, Steve impregnates a local girl, a shadow of the tradition of "Robin Redbreast" (Rodgers, 2017; Huckvale, 2018: 150–52). Both missionaries fall victim to this scheme. There is a wicker tree that is set alight, but it seems to have, in a way that subverts expectations, no sinister function. It's simply a part of May Day. (Beth Boothby does set Sir Lachlan alight, igniting the structure, but this appears to have been an unanticipated rather than a planned immolation.) The movie never received wide theatrical release and hasn't attained cult status.

Another effort to capitalize on the legacy centers on the controversy with David Pinner. Hardy and Shaffer knew his novel *Ritual* and borrowed from it, but Pinner also claimed the story was his, and in 2014 published a second novel following the same theme, titled *The Wicca Woman*.

Figure 15. "Burn the Witch." © X-L Recordings

All of these efforts, which began appearing around the turn of the millennium (even the fanzine *Nuada* started only in 1998), demonstrate that *The Wicker Man* required years to attain its cult status. The fact that British Lion, which never warmed to the film, nevertheless took on its spiritual successor demonstrates an acknowledgment of its fame. *The Wicker Man* has become such a recognized reference that in the animated video for Radiohead's "Burn the Witch," artist Chris Hopewell set up a scenario loosely based on the movie, with its own wicker man. Many other less obvious nods are given in popular culture in the new millennium. *The Wicker Man* is still not mainstream, but it is widely recognized, even if by viewers who quote "Oh no, not the bees! Not the bees!" from the LaBute version. There are *Wicker Man* wikis with stunning detail about the movie. Just as this final manuscript was being submitted, it was announced that Andy Serkis is working on a television adaptation of the movie. Fandom is bound to grow.[2]

As is perhaps fitting for a film never far from conflict, the printed sources for studying this film are often difficult to locate or only available in locations limited to academic readers. Other books on *The Wicker Man* exist, but many of them are priced as collectors' items. A couple of examples will suffice. *Studying* The Wicker Man, by Andy Murray and Lorraine Rolston, is elusive, despite its obvious utility for cinematography courses that discuss the film. A 2003 academic conference titled "*The Wicker Man*: Rituals, Readings and Reactions" led to two books, one of which, according to WorldCat, is only available in 18 libraries worldwide and is not currently available for purchase.[3] (The second book from the conference, *The Quest for* The Wicker Man: *History, Folklore and Pagan Perspectives*, is still available, if priced in inaccessible realms in print format.) Indeed, many resources regarding the movie have become curios in their own right. Their rarity adds to the continuing mystique of *The Wicker Man*. Even the documentary *Burnt Offerings: The Cult of the Wicker Man* (Andrew Abbott and Russell Leven, 2001) remains unavailable in North America.

FINAL THOUGHTS

The Wicker Man remains an enigma. It isn't a perfect film. There are some narrative continuity issues, even in the director's cut. The film doesn't utilize the supernatural; while this may seem a minor point, it's important. Some of the narrative problems, such as Howie breaking into the chemist shop without warrant, are solved only by understanding that the islanders are actually controlling the sergeant's thoughts. The consistency of the narrative also breaks down, as Murray and Rolston point out (2008: 8), when Howie decides to attack Alder MacGregor (Lindsay Kemp) to become Punch in the procession. Clearly this is planned, since the islanders need to get Howie to the site of the faux sacrifice of Rowan Morrison. Lighting the hand of glory (the severed hand lamp—perhaps from the fresh corpse Howie found at the undertaker's which had a bloody stump instead of a hand?) to keep him asleep would only frustrate their plans. How would they know Howie would attack MacGregor if they weren't controlling his thoughts and actions? In other words, the narrative isn't quite as free from the supernatural as most commentators assume. It's very subtle, but the narrative breaks down without it here and there.

The supernatural always lurks in holiday horror. Its recognition as a sub-genre is still relatively new and disagreements exist as to which movies can legitimately be called holiday horror. Does merely taking place on a holiday make a horror film holiday horror? More specific guidelines, such as an ominous history of the day, or the nature of the holiday having an impact on what actually takes place, have been suggested. Horror can happen any day of the year. Holidays have their origins in religions. Most religions assume an unseen world where only specialists can see hidden realities. Holiday horror, whether explicit or not, has the question of the supernatural hanging over it.

If *The Wicker Man* is holiday horror, why wasn't the more mysterious title Beltane (Belthane, as it's spelled in the school register) used more? Since we can't ask those directly involved in the choice, a bit of reasonable speculation may be in order. The true wicker man, as Murray and Rolston suggest (2008: 18), may be Sgt. Howie. With echoes of T. S. Eliot's "Hollow Men," there's a case to be made for their reasoning. "Mayday" became a distress signal around 1920. Although its origin has nothing to do with the holiday (it's based on the French *m'aidez*, "help me"),[4] the fact that the two are homonyms is difficult to miss. The prominent use of May Day in the film may be a hidden call for help by Sgt. Howie. The threat to him, however, isn't so much May Day as celebrated on Summerisle but his own religion, that won't permit others the courtesy of their own beliefs.

NOTES

1. Many of them are recorded in Brown (2000) or in documentaries such as *The Wicker Man Enigma*, or even written out in Paciorek et al. (2018).
2. https://twinfinite.net/2022/10/the-wicker-man-television-in-development-from-andy-serkis/.
3. *Constructing* The Wicker Man: *Film and Cultural Studies Perspectives*, edited by Jonathan Murray and published by the University of Glasgow and Crichton Publications (Dumfries, Scotland) in 2005. WorldCat data may be found here: https://www.worldcat.org/title/constructing-

the-wicker-man-film-and-cultural-studies-perspectives/oclc/70168082&referer=brief_
results#borrow.

4.   See the *Oxford English Dictionary* for details.

BIBLIOGRAPHY

Anthony, David W. and Dorcas R. Brown (1991). "The Origins of Horseback Riding." *Antiquity* 65.246: 22–38.

Aveny, Anthony (2003). *The Book of the Year: A Brief History of Our Seasonal Holidays.* Oxford: Oxford University Press.

Barefoot, Guy (2017). *Trash Cinema: The Lure of the Low. Short Cuts.* London: Wallflower Press.

Bartholomew, David (1977). "*The Wicker Man*: The Story behind the Production of Anthony Shaffer's Occult Masterpiece, the *Citizen Kane* of Horror Films." *Cinefantastique* 6.3: 6–19, 32–47.

Beard, Mary, John North, and Simon Price (1998). *Religions of Rome: Volume 2, A Sourcebook.* Cambridge: Cambridge University Press.

Bellenir, Karen, ed. (2004). *Religious Holidays and Calendars: An Encyclopedic Handbook.* 3rd ed. Detroit: Omnigraphics.

Bidmead, Julye (2004). *The Akitu Festival: Religious Continuity and Royal Legitimation in Mesopotamia.* Piscataway, NJ: Gorgias Press.

Bing, Jonathan (2002). "'Wicker' Horror War Erupts." *Variety*, March 20, 2002. https://variety.com/2002/film/news/wicker-horror-war-erupts-1117864269/ [accessed June 11, 2021].

Blain, Jenny (2011). "Neo-Shamanism: Pagan and 'Neo-Shamanic' Interactions with Archaeology." In *The Oxford Handbook of Archaeology of Ritual and Religion*, edited by Timothy Insoll, 1017–30. New York: Oxford University Press.

Boot, Andy (1996). *Fragments of Fear: An Illustrated History of British Horror Films.* London: Creation Books.

Bord, Janet and Colin Bord (1972). *Mysterious Britain: Ancient Secrets of the United Kingdom and Ireland.* N.p.: The Garnstone Press Ltd.

Brass, Tom (2001). "Reel Images of the Land (Beyond the Forest): Film and the Agrarian Myth." *The Journal of Peasant Studies* 28: 1–56.

Brown, Allan (2000). *Inside* The Wicker Man: *How Not to Make a Cult Classic.* London: Pan Macmillan.

Byron, Stuart (1977). "The Industry: Something Wicker This Way Comes." *Film Comment* 13.6: 29–31.

————. (1978). "Back Talk." *Film Comment* 14.2: 78–79.

Cabell, Craig (2006). *Witchfinder General: The Biography of Matthew Hopkins.* Stroud: Sutton.

Caesar, Julius (1915). *Caesar's Commentaries.* Translated by W. A. Macdevitt. Everyman's Library.

Carden, Maren Lockwood (1998). *Oneida: Utopian Community to Modern Corporation.* Syracuse: Syracuse University Press.

Catterall, Ali and Simon Wells (2001). *Your Face Here: British Cult Movies since the Sixties.* London: Fourth Estate.

Chadwick, Nora (1971). *The Celts.* London: Penguin.

Chambers, Robert (1864). *The Book of Days: A Miscellany of Popular Antiquities in Connection with the Calendar.* 2 volumes. London: W. & R. Chambers.

Clover, Carol J. (2015). *Men, Women, and Chain Saws: Gender in the Modern Horror Film.* Princeton: Princeton University Press.

Collier, John Payne (2006). *Punch and Judy: A Short History with the Original Dialogue.* New York: Dover.

Cooper, Ian (2011). *Witchfinder General.* Devil's Advocates. Leighton Buzzard: Auteur.

Cowan, Douglas E. (2020). "'So we're just going to ignore the bear': Imagining Religion at Midsommar." *Journal of Gods and Monsters* 1: 54–56.

————. (2021). *The Forbidden Body: Sex, Horror, and the Religious Imagination.* New York: New York University Press.

Cunliffe, Barry (1997). *The Ancient Celts*. Oxford: Oxford University Press.

Decker, Lindsay (2021). *Transnationalism and Genre Hybridity in New British Horror Cinema*. Horror Studies. Cardiff: University of Wales Press.

DeRogatis, Amy (2014). *Saving Sex: Sexuality and Salvation in Christian Evangelicalism*. New York: Oxford University Press.

Ellis, Bill (2000). *Raising the Devil: Satanism, New Religions, and the Media*. Lexington: University Press of Kentucky.

Ellis, Peter Berresford (2002). *A Brief History of the Druids*. Philadelphia: Running Press.

Endsjø, Dag Øistein (2011). *Sex and Religion: Teachings and Taboos in the History of World Faiths*. London: Reaktion Books.

Evans-Powell, David (2021). *The Blood on Satan's Claw*. Devil's Advocates. Liverpool: Auteur/Liverpool University Press.

Forbes, Bruce David (2015). *America's Favorite Holidays: Candid Histories*. Oakland: University of California Press.

Franks, Benjamin, Stephen Harper, Jonathan Murray, and Lesley Stevenson, eds. (2007). *The Quest for* The Wicker Man: *History, Folklore and Pagan Perspectives*. Edinburgh: Luath Press.

Frazer, J. G. (1913). *The Golden Bough: A Study in Magic and Religion*. Part VII, Balder the Beautiful. 3rd ed. London: Macmillan and Co.

Freeland, Cynthia A. (2000). *The Naked and the Undead: Evil and the Appeal of Horror*. Boulder: Westview.

Gibson, Marion (2013a). *Imagining the Pagan Past: Gods and Goddesses in Literature and History since the Dark Ages*. Abingdon: Routledge.

———. (2013b). "Wicker Men and Straw Dogs: Internal Colonialism in Celtic Novels and Films 1968–1978." *National Identities* 15.2: 139–56.

Giesberg, Judith (2017). *Sex and the Civil War: Soldiers, Pornography, and the Making of American Morality*. Chapel Hill: University of North Carolina Press.

Goldberg, B. Z. (1930). *The Sacred Fire: The Story of Sex in Religion*. New York: Horace Liveright.

Grafius, Brandon (2020). *The Witch*. Devil's Advocates. Liverpool: Auteur/Liverpool University Press.

Green, Miranda (2011). *The Gods of the Celts*. Stroud: The History Press.

Halberstam, Judith (1995). *Skin Shows: Gothic Horror and the Technology of Monsters*. Durham, NC: Duke University Press.

Hardy, Robin and Anthony Shaffer (1978). *The Wicker Man*. New York: Three Rivers Press.

Heller-Nicholas, Alexandra (2019). *Masks in Horror Cinema: Eyes without Faces*. Horror Studies. Cardiff: University of Wales Press.

Homans, George Casper (1970). *English Villagers of the Thirteenth Century*. New York: Harper Torchbooks.

Huckvale, David (2018). *A Green and Pagan Land: Myth, Magic and Landscape in British Film and Television*. Jefferson, NC: McFarland.

Hutchings, Peter (2021). *Hammer and Beyond: The British Horror Film*. Manchester: Manchester University Press.

Hutton, Ronald (1991). *The Pagan Religions of the Ancient British Isles*. Oxford: Blackwell Publishers.

————. (1996). *Stations of the Sun: A History of the Ritual Year in Britain*. Oxford: Oxford University Press.

————. (1999). *The Triumph of the Moon: A History of Modern Pagan Witchcraft*. Oxford: Oxford University Press.

————. (2011). *Blood and Mistletoe: The History of the Druids in Britain*. New Haven: Yale University Press.

Ingebretsen, Edward J. (2001). *At Stake: Monsters and the Rhetoric of Fear in Public Culture*. Chicago: University of Chicago Press.

Ingham, Howard David (2018). *We Don't Go Back: A Watcher's Guide to Folk Horror*. Swansea: Room 207 Press.

Johnston, Derek (2015). *Haunted Seasons: Television Ghost Stories for Christmas and Horror for Halloween*. Palgrave Gothic. New York: Palgrave Macmillan.

Kelly, Aidan (2017). "About Naming Ostara, Litha, and Mabon." *Including Paganism*, May 2, 2017. https://www.patheos.com/blogs/aidankelly/2017/05/naming-ostara-litha-mabon/ [accessed October 18, 2021].

Krzywinska, Tanya (2000). *A Skin for Dancing in: Possession, Witchcraft and Voodoo in Film*. Trowbridge: Flicks Books.

———. (2006). *Sex and the Cinema*. London: Wallflower Press.

Lin, Erika T. (2015). "A Witch in the Morris: Hobbyhorse Tricks and Early Modern Erotic Transformations." In *The Oxford Handbook of Dance and Theater*, edited by Nadine George-Graves, 335–69. New York: Oxford University Press.

Lynch, Michael (1991). *Scotland: A New History*. London: Century.

Magie, David (1924). *Historia Augusta, Volume II*. Loeb Classical Library, volume 140. Cambridge, MA: Harvard University Press.

Magliocco, Sabina (2003). *Witching Culture: Folklore and Neo-Paganism in America*. Philadelphia: University of Pennsylvania Press.

Marcus, Steven (2017). *The Other Victorians: A Study of Sexuality and Pornography in Mid-Nineteenth-Century England*. Abingdon: Routledge.

McDonagh, Maitland (2002). "Tales from the Crypt." *Film Comment* 38.5: 66–69.

McGookin, Colin (1998). "Labyrinthine Parades." *Fortnight* 372: 26–27.

Morton, Lisa (2012). *Trick or Treat: A History of Halloween*. London: Reaktion.

Moss, Candida (2014). *The Myth of Persecution: How Early Christians Invented the Story of Martyrdom*. San Francisco: HarperOne.

Murray, Andy and Lorraine Rolston (2008). *Studying The Wicker Man*. Studying Films. Leighton Buzzard: Auteur.

Murray, Jonathan, ed. (2005). *Constructing The Wicker Man: Film and Cultural Studies Perspectives*. Dumfries: University of Glasgow, Crichton Publications.

NicDhàna, Kathryn Price, Erynn Rowan Laurie, C. Lee Vermeers, and Kym Lambert ní Dhoireann (2007). *The CR FAQ: An Introduction to Celtic Reconstructionist Paganism*. Leverett, MA: River House Publishing.

Nissinen, Martti and Risto Uro, eds. (2008). *Sacred Marriages: The Divine-Human Sexual Metaphor from Sumer to Early Christianity*. Winona Lake, IN: Eisenbrauns.

Otto, Rudolf (1922). *The Idea of the Holy*. Oxford: Oxford University Press.

Paciorek, Andy, Grey Malkin, Richard Hing, and Katherine Peach, eds. (2018). *Folk Horror Revival: Field Studies*. Durham, UK: Wyrd Harvest Press.

Pettitt, Tom (2005). "When the Golden Bough Breaks: Folk Drama and the Theatre Historian." *Nordic Journal of English Studies* 4.2: 1–40.

Phillips, Kendall R. (2018). *A Place of Darkness: The Rhetoric of Horror in Early American Cinema*. Austin: University of Texas Press.

Rhodes, Gary D. (2018). *The Birth of the American Horror Film*. Edinburgh: Edinburgh University Press.

Rodgers, D. (2017). "Robin Redbreast and BBC's Play for Today: 1970's Folk Horror for Christmas." In *Yuletide Terror: Christmas Horror on Film and Television*, edited by Paul Corupe and Kier-La Janisse, 156–69. Toronto: Spectacular Optical Publications.

Roper, Lyndal (2004). *Witch Craze: Terror and Fantasy in Baroque Germany*. New Haven: Yale University Press.

Rothery, David A. (2015). *Moons: A Very Short Introduction*. Oxford: Oxford University Press.

Russell, Jeffrey B. and Brooks Alexander (2007). *A History of Witchcraft: Sorcerers, Heretics and Pagans*. London: Thames & Hudson.

Schwartz, Howard (1988). *Lilith's Cave: Jewish Tales of the Supernatural*. New York: Oxford University Press.

Scovell, Adam (2017). *Folk Horror: Hours Dreadful and Things Strange*. Leighton Buzzard: Auteur.

Smith, Wilfred Cantwell (1991). *The Meaning and End of Religion*. Minneapolis: Fortress Press.

Sopher, Philip (2014). "Where the Five-Day Workweek Came From." *The Atlantic*, August 21, 2014. https://www.theatlantic.com/business/archive/2014/08/where-the-five-day-workweek-came-from/378870/ [accessed December 27, 2021].

Todorov, Tzvetan and Richard M. Berrong (1976). "The Origin of Genres." *New Literary History* 8.1: 159–70.

Tudor, Andrew (1974). *Theories of Film*. London: Secker and Warburg.

Urban, Hugh B. (2006). *Magia Sexualis: Sex, Magic, and Liberation in Modern Western Esotericism*. Berkeley: University of California Press.

Vander Kaay, Chris and Kathleen Fernandez-Vander Kaay (2016). *Horror Films by Subgenre: A Viewer's Guide*. Jefferson, NC: McFarland.

Wagemakers, Bart (2010). "Incest, Infanticide, and Cannibalism: Anti-Christian Imputations in the Roman Empire." *Greece & Rome* 57.2: 337–54.

Wainwright, Martin (2007). *The Guardian Book of April Fool's Day*. London: Aurum Press.

Wiggins, Steve A. (2018). *Holy Horror: The Bible and Fear in Movies*. Jefferson, NC: McFarland.

Young, Rob (2010). *Electric Eden: Unearthing Britain's Visionary Music*. New York: Farrar, Straus and Giroux.

WEBSITES

https://twinfinite.net/2022/10/the-wicker-man-television-in-development-from-andy-serkis/ [accessed October 12, 2022].

https://twm.fandom.com/wiki/Props#Book_about_May_Day_in_the_library_Howie_reads.C2.A0 [accessed December 4, 2021].

https://twm.fandom.com/wiki/The_Wicker_Man_(1973)_Wikia [accessed November 28, 2021].

https://web.archive.org/web/20120815142641/http://anglopolish.com/index.php/en/archive/29-polish-tradition/155-international-workers-day-may-day [accessed November 16, 2021].

https://www.telegraph.co.uk/news/uknews/1486529/Traditional-songs-beat-the-happy-clappers-hands-down-in-search-for-Britains-best-hymns.html [accessed June 10, 2021].

https://www.worldcat.org/title/constructing-the-wicker-man-film-and-cultural-studies-perspectives/oclc/70168082&referer=brief_results#borrow [accessed October 4, 2021].